2025 Global Mission Literature Association

사막길을 걷는 이에게 들려주는 노래
Rose of the Desert

아데니움

국제 문학사

주제 시

아데니움

김동욱

절망을 뚫고 피어나는 꽃을 보았습니다
살갗 마저 타올라 버려져도 고독한 만큼
아름답고 버린 만큼 일어서는 꽃,
아픈 만큼 돋아나는 부활의 꽃을 보았습니다

갈보리 버려짐의 언덕에서도 잠들지 않은
소망의 꽃을 보았습니다
아련하게 떠오르는 사막의 장미꽃
아데니움, 마른 만큼 향기 내는 아데니움
고통의 절벽에서 꽃봉우리 피어 내는
사막의 장미를 보았습니다

난 아직도 잠들지 않았다고 숨 쉬고 있다고
절망은 이르다고 영혼의 절망을 보듬고
하늘 꽃 전해주는 아데니움 꽃을 보았습니다

김동욱 시인 선교사는 글로벌 선교회 문학회를 섬기며, 한국예술인 복지재단 회원, 참빛 국제 교회 담임으로 현지 목회를 하고 있다. 저서로 "하늘 기도" " 오매 햇빛 들 것다" 외

Theme Poem

Adenium
Kim Dong-ouk

I saw a flower break through despair,
Burned and withered, yet rising in air.
Lonely yet lovely, forsaken yet strong,
A bloom of revival, where sorrows belong.

On Calvary's hill, where silence grew deep,
A flower of hope refused to sleep.
Through thorns and ashes, still it grows,
Adenium—the desert rose.
Faintly it glows in the withering sand,
Fragrant with thirst in a barren land.

From cliffs of sorrow, its petals unwind,
A bloom that whispers, "I will not decline."
"I still breathe, I will not fall,
Despair is fleeting, not fate at all."

죽음의 겨울이 지나가고 봄이 다가와
마른 가지 속에 꿈틀대는 생명의 봉우리를
보았습니다. 추운 밤을 견디며 강해진 봉우리,
버린 만큼 일어서는 가시눈꽃을 보았습니다

아픈 만큼 돋아나는 의지의 꽃
바람 속에 피어나는 새로운 삶 눈물 뒤에
빛을 찾는 아름다움을 보았습니다

지쳐 쓰러져도 다시 일어나
온몸에 피어오르는 강한 불꽃,
깊이 숨긴 꿈들을 세상에 펼쳐
두 날개를 펴고서 날아오르는
부활의 노래를 들었습니다

아 아련하게 떠오르는 아데니움,
짓밟힐수록 고운 영혼의 노래
너와 나의 노래, 아데니움!

Embracing the wounds, it lifts its head,
A flower that speaks where souls have bled.
Winter fades, and spring draws near,
Life stirs within the branches bare.

Through bitter nights, the bud stands tall,
Rising again from what was small.
Thorns may wound, but still it grows,
A flame in the wind, a light that glows.
Tears may fall, yet hope will rise,
Adenium, reaching for the skies.

Though trampled down, it sings anew,
A melody pure, both yours and mine too.
Spreading its wings in the dawn's embrace,
Adenium—beauty in grace.

차 례

주제 시 / 아데니움 / 김동욱 시인　　　　　　　　　　　2
글로벌선교문학회 어제와 오늘　　　　　　　　　　　9
첫 동인지를 출판하며 / 김동욱 목사　　　　　　　　12
동인지 출판을 축하드리며 / 이영희 목사　　　　　　16
사막의 장미, 아데니움을 축복하며 /김성구 박사　　20
글로벌선교문학회 연혁 및 사역 소개 / 김동욱 목사　22
다시 걷는 길, "아데니움" 간증 / 이신헌 목사　　　　28

동인 작가 글

■고승희
고자질　　　　　　　　　　　　　　　　　　　　40
생명의 길, 혈관의 노래　　　　　　　　　　　　42
나의 몸, 성스러운 선교지　　　　　　　　　　　46

■고정옥
십가가.2　　　　　　　　　　　　　　　　　　　50
로뎀나무 아래서　　　　　　　　　　　　　　　52
엄마는 꽃을 무척 좋아합니다　　　　　　　　　56

■김동욱
흔들리는 바나나 잎　　　　　　　　　　　　　　62
신앙 시의 목소리　　　　　　　　　　　　　　　66
크리스쳔 작가가 되는 첫걸음　　　　　　　　　70

■김제순
소나기　　　　　　　　　　　　　　　　　　　　74
십자가　　　　　　　　　　　　　　　　　　　　78
몽상으로　　　　　　　　　　　　　　　　　　　88

■김진순
어느 봄날의 장터　　　　　　　　　　　　　82
내가 선택한 평안　　　　　　　　　　　　　84
노년의 행복　　　　　　　　　　　　　　　90

■노희설
심연　　　　　　　　　　　　　　　　　　　96
바람　　　　　　　　　　　　　　　　　　　98
내 생애 가장 소중한 선물　　　　　　　　100

■문미숙
주여 오늘도　　　　　　　　　　　　　　108
인생은 품앗이란다　　　　　　　　　　　110
살균소독, 오병이어　　　　　　　　　　　118

■박상금
목자의 기도　　　　　　　　　　　　　　124
기억하니 이쁜 딸들아　　　　　　　　　126
네 눈물 위해 내가 죽었노라　　　　　　130

■박혜원
햇살이 놀자 하네　　　　　　　　　　　138
하나님의 깜짝 선물 우쿨렐레　　　　　140
나의 천국 여행기　　　　　　　　　　　146

■이미셀
동행　　　　　　　　　　　　　　　　　154
Northern Island Life　　　　　　　　　　158
원주민과 Denturist　　　　　　　　　　164

■이정희
벚꽃 앤딩　　　　　　　　　　　　　　　170
러시아를 위한 기도　　　　　　　　　　172
러시아에서 만난 평양 손님　　　　　　174

■이진종
어떤 길   182
구십 구 도   184
캐나다 원주민 사역을 하면서   192

■이현경
둥지   200
벼랑 끝에서   202
미래의 어느 날 활짝 피어날 손주들에게   204

■전에스더
작은 것들의 소중함을 잊지 않게 하소서   212
22년의 친구, 내 안경   214
잃어버린 것과 얻는 것   220

■정재식
믿음의 승리   228
나의 소명   230
고요한 순례자의 길   232

■조복미
친 구   240
네 모습도 그리 아름답단다   242
그리운 나의 어머니   250

■홍연옥
초록 벌레와 내 영혼   256
그리움의 무게   260
오늘은 네 노트에서 네 글씨를 만져 보았단다   262

■글로벌선교문학회 어제와 오늘■

글로벌선교문학회 창설 후 첫 문학 캠프

제1회 "시와 찬미의 향연"을 마치고 출연진들

■제1회, 2회 글로벌선교문학회 예술제■

모두의 위로가 필요하여 특별하게 초대받은 선교사님들

선교사 및 현지 목회자 150명을 초대하여 복음 가수 전용대 목사 찬양팀과 콜라보를 이루어 위로의 예술제를 가졌습니다.

첫 동인지 출판을 하며

김동욱/ 글로벌선교문학회 대표

지나온 삼 년의 발걸음이 그리 쉽지는 않았습니다.
 각자에게 주어진 선교의 분주한 현장 속에서 작은 시간을 어떻게 효과적이고 창조적이며 의미 있게 사용할 것인가? 일상의 현장을 보다 새롭게 하고 연합하여 더 큰 시너지를 나타낼 무엇이 없을 것인가? 많은 시간을 기도하며 고민하는 가운데 글로벌선교문학회(Global Mission Literature Association)의 첫걸음을 내디뎠습니다.

 2025년 처음 도전하는 동인지 출판을 통해 사막의 길을 걷고 있는 분들에게 현재 걷고 있는 그 길이 분명 의미 있는 길임을 주께서 전하기 원하셨습니다. 코로나 이후 많은 순례의 길을 걷는 분들이 사막과 같은 험하고 외롭고 절망적인 길을 걷고 있지만, 그 길 가운데도 분명히 함께 하시는 하늘 아버지의 메시지를 전하고 싶었습니다. 사막의 장미꽃 "아데니움"의 소망을 함께 나누고 싶었습니다. 그리하여 지난 1년 동안 글을 쓰며, 워십댄스를 연습하며, 책을 만들며, 올릴 무대를 꿈꾸며 한 걸음 한 걸음 걸어왔습니다.

Words of dedication
"May continue to bring the joy of morning manna to all pilgrims"

Kim Dong Ouk
-President of the Global Mission Literature Association-

The past three years have not been without challenge. In the midst of the busyness each of us faces in our respective mission fields, we found ourselves asking: How might we use the fragmented pieces of time in a way that is meaningful, creative, and effective? Is there not something that could renew our everyday moments, draw us together, and ignite a greater synergy?

In prayer and deep reflection over such questions, the first steps of the Global Mission Literature Association were taken.

Through this first attempt at publishing a literary journal in 2025, it was our earnest desire that those walking the desert paths of life might hear from the Lord Himself that the road they now travel is indeed a meaningful one. Since the days of the pandemic, many pilgrims have found themselves on harsh, lonely, and despairing roads. Yet even there, we believe, the message of our Heavenly Father still resounds — He walks with us. We wished to share the hope of the desert rose, Adenium, blooming in arid places. Thus, for the past year, we have written, practiced worship dance, prepared the book, and envisioned the stage upon which this offering might be placed. Step by step, we have walked this journey.

지난 3년 동안 줌 강의를 통해 창작의 샘을 퍼 올리신 아데니움 동인 작가 17명을 축하드립니다. 어려운 길을 해 내셨습니다. 장하십니다. 시니어 선교사역 중 사막 한가운데 쓰러져 더 이상 걸을 수 없는 상황으로 철수했지만 사막에도 분명히 길이 있음을 믿고 수천의 밤을 눈물과 기도와 재활의지로 불태워 다시 일어서셔서 출판 기념식 무대에 멋지게 서신 이신헌 목사님과 곁에서 헌신의 길을 걸어오신 박효영 사모님께 박수와 존경의 인사를 전합니다.

아울러, 첫 동인지 '아데니움'이 세상에 빛을 볼 수 있도록 여러 가지로 후원해 주시고 축하의 글과 평론을 써주신 국제문학 발행인 김성구 박사님께 깊은 감사를 드립니다.

아데니움 꽃이 사막의 길을 걷는 이들에게 희망을 주기까지는 수억의 밤을 목마름과 외로움 속에서 지새운 결과입니다. 저희 글로벌선교문학회 (GMLA) 가 지구촌 곳곳에서 사막과 같은 선교지를 걸으며 지상에서의 사명을 감당하시는 모든 순례자들께 아침이슬 같은 만나의 기쁨을 지속적으로 전할 수 있기를 소망합니다.

Congratulations to the 17 Adenium Writers Who Drew from the Well of Creativity Through Three Years of Zoom Lectures.

You have walked a difficult path, and you have done it well. We honor you.

To Rev. Shinheon Lee, who, in the midst of senior missionary service, collapsed in the heart of the desert and was forced to withdraw—yet rose again by faith that even in the desert, a path exists—having burned through thousands of nights in tears, prayer, and the will to rehabilitate: we celebrate you. And to Pastor Hyo-young Park, who faithfully walked the path of devotion beside him, we offer our heartfelt applause and deep respect.

We also extend our sincere gratitude to Dr. Sung-Goo Kim, publisher of International Literature, who supported this first literary journal Adenium in many ways, and who contributed his congratulations and literary critique, helping it see the light of day.

The bloom of the Adenium flower—offering hope to those walking desert roads—is the fruit of countless nights endured in thirst and solitude. It is our sincere hope that the Global Mission Literature Association (GMLA) may continue to bring the joy of morning manna to all pilgrims faithfully fulfilling their earthly calling in the desert-like mission fields across the globe.

동인지 출판을 축하 드리며

이영희 목사(변화프로젝트 교도소 문서선교 대표, ICLTC 설립자)

첫 동인지 출판을 진심으로 축하드리며, 글로벌선교문학회의 모든 수고하신 분들께 찬양과 박수를 보냅니다.

예수님은 우리를 누구보다 잘 아십니다. "나는 포도나무요 너희는 가지라. 그가 내 안에, 내가 그 안에 거하면 사람이 열매를 많이 맺나니 나를 떠나서는 너희가 아무 것도 할 수 없음이라." (요한복음 15:5)

예수님이 함께하시지 않았다면 이번 출판은 불가능했을 것입니다. 성령님의 인도하심과 치유의 역사, 그리고 영성 창작 아카데미를 통해 비전을 품고 섬김과 열정으로 이끌어주신 김동욱 선교사님의 헌신이 아름다운 열매를 맺게 하셨습니다.

믿음과 사역의 여정 속에서 선교사님들과 사역자들의 이야기를 만나는 것은 하나님의 놀라우신 은혜입니다. 주님을 사랑하는 마음으로 최선을 다해 써 내려간, 마음 깊은 곳의 고난과 아픔, 눈물, 그리고 하나님과의 여정과 치유가 담긴 글들은 독자들의 마음을 깊이 울립니다.

Warm Congratulations on the Publication of Your First Literary Anthology

Rev. Younghee Lee (Director of the Transformation Project Prison Literature Ministry, Founder of ICLTC)

I offer my heartfelt congratulations on the publication of your very first literary anthology. Praise and heartfelt applause to everyone at the Global Mission Literature Association who poured their time, love, and effort into this work.

Jesus knows us better than anyone. As He said,
"I am the vine, you are the branches. If you remain in me and I in you, you will bear much fruit; apart from me you can do nothing." (John 15:5)

Without Jesus, this publication would not have been possible. It is only through the guidance of the Holy Spirit, His healing work, and Academy the vision nurtured through the Spiritual creative that this beautiful fruit was borne—thanks to the servant-hearted leadership and passionate dedication of Missionary Donguk Kim.

To encounter the stories of missionaries and ministers in the journey of faith and ministry is to witness God's amazing grace. Written with sincerity and a heart full of love for the Lord, these pieces—woven with pain, trials, tears, and moments of healing in God's presence—are sure to touch the hearts of readers deeply.

성령님께서 사용하셔서, 이 책은 세상에 주님의 놀라우심을 알리고 상처를 치유하며, 예수님의 사랑을 전하는 귀한 도구가 될 것입니다. 여러분의 믿음과 사역의 부르심과 간증의 글은 하나님의 살아계심을 드러내며, 성령님께서 여러분의 글을 통해 하나님의 계획과 치유를 세상에 전하게 하실 것입니다.

이 책에 담긴 모든 글에는 하나님에 대한 사랑이 깃들어 있습니다. 그리고 그 사랑은 이미 주님의 사랑을 입은 증거입니다.

주님은 우리가 상상할 수 없는 길로 가장 좋은 길로 인도하십니다. 좋은 멘토를 따라간다는 것은 여정에 있어 큰 축복입니다. 김동욱 선교사님의 섬세한 지도를 통해 여러분의 글이 세상에 주님의 빛을 밝히 드러내게 된 것 또한, 주님께 큰 기쁨이 되리라 믿습니다.

다시 한번, 첫 동인지 출판을 진심으로 축하드리며, 하나님께 모든 영광을 올려드립니다.

May the Holy Spirit use this book as a precious instrument —to proclaim the wonders of the Lord to the world, to bring healing to the wounded, and to share the deep love of Jesus. The faith, calling, and testimonies expressed in your writing bear witness to the living God. Through your words, the Holy Spirit will surely reveal God's plans and healing to many.

Every page of this book carries the fragrance of love for God. And that love itself is a beautiful testimony that you have already been embraced by the love of Christ.

The Lord leads us in ways far beyond what we could ever imagine—always towards what is best. To follow a good mentor is a great blessing on life's journey. I truly believe that through the gentle guidance of Missionary Kim, your writing has become a shining light of the Lord in this world, bringing joy to His heart.

Once again, I warmly congratulate you on the publication of your first anthology, and I give all the glory to God.

사막의 장미, 『아데니움』을 축복하며

문학평론가, 국제문학 발행인 시인 김성구 박사

"사막에도 꽃은 피어납니다".
 그 고요하고도 메마른 길을 묵묵히 걷는 이들이 있었기에, 오늘 우리는 『아데니움』이라는 이름으로 피어난 문학의 꽃을 마주하게 되었습니다.
 글로벌선교문학회는 지난 3년간 '문학과 예술로 복음을 전한다'는 거룩한 비전을 품고, 순례의 걸음을 걸어왔습니다. 그 여정은 결코 쉽지 않았지만, Zoom 강의실에서, 찬양의 무대에서, 워십댄스의 몸짓과 오카리나의 숨결 속에서, 창작의 언어로 피어난 '아데니움'은 영적 사막을 걷는 이들에게 새로운 생명의 향기를 전하고자 하였습니다.
 이 책은 단순한 동인이 아닙니다.
 절망의 밤을 지나 다시 걸음을 내딛은 이들의 고백이자, 선교사들의 눈물과 기도가 응결된 살아 있는 문학입니다. 그리고 이 문학은 고백으로 머물지 않고, 하나님의 임재를 증언하는 예배의 형식으로까지 확장되어, 하나의 선교 축제가 되었습니다.
 『아데니움』은 선교 문학이라는 생소할 수 있는 영역에서, 창작과 영성을 조화롭게 엮어낸 값진 결실입니다. 각 편에 담긴 시와 수필, 간증과 회복의 이야기는 단순한 기록이 아니라, "그럼에도 불구하고 주님을 찬양하라"는 믿음의 외침입니다.
 이 귀한 첫 결실에 참여하신 동인 작가들, 문학 수업을 인도하고 문학회를 섬겨온 김동욱 선교사님, 그리고 다시 일어나 아데니움의 이름처럼 복음의 무대에 선 선교사님들께 존경과 박수를 보냅니다.
 『아데니움』은 앞으로도 사막을 걷는 모든 순례자들에게, 아침 이슬 같은 만나가 되어줄 것입니다. 그리고 이 동인지를 시작으로, 글로벌선교문학회가 세계 문학의 한가운데서 복음의 향기를 더욱 널리 전하길 기대합니다.
 고난을 딛고 피어난 꽃 한 송이,
 그 안에 담긴 부활의 노래와 소망을 기꺼이 축복합니다.

Blessings upon the Desert Rose, Adenium

Literary Critic & Publisher of International Literature Dr. Sung-goo Kim

Even in the desert, flowers bloom.
Because there were those who silently walked that quiet and arid path, today we are able to behold a literary flower blossoming under the name Adenium.
Over the past three years, the Global Mission Literature Association has journeyed forward with the sacred vision of "proclaiming the gospel through literature and the arts." It has not been an easy path, yet through Zoom classrooms, worship stages, the motions of worship dance, and the breath of the ocarina, Adenium has bloomed in the language of creation, bringing the fragrance of new life to those walking through spiritual deserts.
This book is not merely a literary journal.
It is the confession of those who, after nights of despair, dared to take another step forward. It is a living testimony, condensed with the tears and prayers of missionaries. And this literature does not remain merely as personal expression; it expands into a form of worship that testifies to the presence of God—becoming a festival of missions.
Adenium is a precious fruit, harmonizing creativity and spirituality within the often unfamiliar realm of mission literature. The poems, essays, testimonies, and stories of healing contained in these pages are more than records—they are faith-filled cries that proclaim, "Yet will I praise the Lord."
To the contributing writers of this treasured first volume, to Missionary Dongwook Kim who has faithfully led the literature classes and served the association, and to the missionaries who have risen again to stand on the stage of the gospel, like the name Adenium, we extend our deepest respect and heartfelt applause.
Adenium will continue to be a dew-like manna for all pilgrims walking through the desert. And with this inaugural publication, we look forward to the Global Mission Literature Association spreading the fragrance of the gospel more widely at the very heart of world literature.
A single flower that bloomed through suffering—
within it, we wholeheartedly bless the song of resurrection and the hope it contains.

글로벌선교문학회 연혁 및 사역 소개

　　Global Mission Literature Association(GMLA) 는 2023년 2월 문학을 통해 종합 예술 선교를 지향하며 오래 기도해 온 시인 김동욱 선교사를 중심으로 한 선교사 12명이 발족하였습니다. 문화 예술 선교 사역은 언어와 문화를 초월한 글로벌로의 선교 사역으로의 믿음을 갖고 첫 단계로 <선교 문학 창작 클래스>를 시작하였습니다. 주1 회 줌 클래스를 통해 문학창작의 기초부터 시작하였으며 GMLA안에 <워십댄스 팀인 에이레네>와 <오카리나 연주팀 시르오르: 빛의 노래> 팀을 두어 연습한 결과 2023년 10월 글로벌선교문학회 1회 " 시와 찬미의 향연"으로 무대에 올렸습니다. 70여명의 선교사들을 초청하여 준비한 창작 시 낭독와 찬양, 워십 댄스로 하나님께 영광을 돌렸습니다.

　2024년 들어 이영희 목사님이 운영하는 <영성훈련 프로젝트 커뮤니케이션> 회원 15명을 대상으로 한 < 2기 선교 문학 창작 기초반>을 열었습니다. 첫 시작한 클래스는 중급반으로 조절하여 기초반과 함께 주 2회, 중급반 화(저녁 9시), 기초반 목(오전 10시)을 열어 현재에 이르고 있으며, 워십댄스 팀은 주 1,2회 모여 새로운 워십댄스 곡을 연습하고, 시르오르 또한 주 1회 모여 오카리나 연주를 연습합니다.

History and Ministry of the Global Mission Literature Association (GMLA)

The Global Mission Literature Association (GMLA) was established in February 2023, birthed through prayer and a shared vision of holistic arts ministry through literature. Led by missionary and poet Rev. Dongwook Kim, twelve like-minded missionaries came together with the calling to pursue global mission beyond borders of language and culture through the medium of literature and the arts. With faith in God's global redemptive purpose, the GMLA launched its first initiative: the "Missionary Creative Writing Class." Meeting weekly over Zoom, participants began with foundational training in literary writing. Within GMLA, two ministry teams were also formed: "Eirene," a worship dance team, and "Si'or: Song of Light," an ocarina ensemble. After months of preparation, these teams presented their first showcase in October 2023:

"An Evening of Poetry and Praise"—a worship celebration that brought together original poetry readings, praise music, and worship dance, all to glorify God. Over 70 missionaries were invited to the event, which served as a sacred offering of artistic worship.

In 2024, in collaboration with Rev. Younghee Lee's Spiritual Formation Communication Project, GMLA launched its second cohort of the Missionary Creative Writing Class, welcoming 15 new participants. The program now offers two levels: an intermediate class (Tuesdays at 9 p.m.) and a foundational class (Thursdays at 10 a.m.) both continuing to nurture the creative gifts of missionaries. The worship dance team meets weekly to prepare new choreography, and the Si'Ore ensemble gathers weekly for ocarina practice.

2024년 10월 제 2회 " 시와 찬미의 향연"을 복음가수 전용대 목사님 일행과 함께 선교 자녀 학교인 페이스 아카데미에서 위로와 새 힘이 필요한 한국 선교사 가정 및 현지 목회자 가정에서 150명을 초대하여 " 너 물가로 나오라" 라는 제목으로 시낭독, 워십댄스, 복음송 축제를 열었습니다.

창단 3년 째인 2025년은, 동인지 출판 및 출판기념 예술제를 목표로 일년 동안 준비를 하였습니다. 사막같은 연단과 고통의 길을 통과한 후 다시 피어나는 내용이 담긴 " 아데니움: 사막의 장미꽃 The Rose of Desert"를 주제로 하여 18명의 동인 작가들이 오랫동안 학습하며 창작품을 쓰고 있습니다.

Looking ahead, the Second Annual "Evening of Poetry and Praise" is scheduled for October 2024. In partnership with gospel singer Rev. Yongdae Jeon and his team, this worship event—titled "Come to the Waters"—will take place at Faith Academy, a school for missionary children. The gathering will invite 150 participants, including Korean missionary families and local pastoral families, to be refreshed and encouraged through poetry, worship dance, and gospel music.

As the Global Mission Literature Association (GMLA) enters its third year in 2025, we have prayerfully prepared for a milestone: the publication of our first anthology and a celebratory arts festival to mark the occasion. Under the theme "Adenium: The Rose of the Desert," 18 dedicated missionary writers have journeyed through a season of deep learning and reflection, crafting original works birthed from the trials and refinements of desert-like hardship—stories of hope reborn after suffering.

워십댄스 팀과 시르오르팀의 오카리나 연습, 특별히 국내 목회 조기 은퇴후 시니어 선교사로 필리핀에 와서 8년 동안 선교 사역을 열정적으로 하다가, 건강 검진위해 국내 들어가 뇌경색으로 쓰러져 4년 동안의 길고 긴 인내의 터널을 지나 다시 사막의 장미꽃처럼 일어 서서 복음을 전하는 이신헌 목사님과 박효영 사모님의 간증과 재정 후원, 창작곡인 아데니움 노래에 맞춰 워십댄스를 준비하여 무대를 빛내주고 이경 사모님의 헌신으로 풍성한 동인지 출판 기념 예술제가 펼쳐지게 됩니다.

글로벌선교문학회는 문화예술 사역을 통해 언어와 문화의 장벽을 뛰어넘은 보다 넓고 깊은 선교의 무기를 들고 글로벌을 향해 나가기를 소망합니다. 현재 30여명의 멤버가 같은 목표를 위해 마음을 모아 매일 창작의 시간을 보내고 있습니다. 이를 위해서는 보다 깊은 영성과 전문성을 가진 선교 마인드 멤버가 필요하고, 겸손과 진실, 영성으로 연합한 협력이 요구됩니다.

이를 위한 재정 후원과 기도후원도 필요하므로 직접 간접적으로 참여하기 원하시는 분들의 많은 관심 부탁 드립니다.

Our worship dance team and Sir Or: Song of Light ocarina ensemble have also faithfully practiced to offer their best in worship. A particularly moving highlight will be the testimony of Rev. Shinheon Lee and Mrs. Hyoyoung Park, who served passionately in the Philippines as senior missionaries after early retirement from pastoral ministry in Korea. After returning to Korea for a medical checkup, Rev. Lee suffered a severe stroke and endured a long four-year journey of pain and perseverance. Now, like a rose blooming in the desert, he stands again to proclaim the gospel. Their story of endurance and resurrection in Christ, their financial needs, and their participation in our event will be a testament to God's faithfulness.

They will also present a worship dance to the original song "Adenium", created especially for this event. Through the devoted support of Mrs. Kyung Lee, our anthology launch and celebratory arts festival will be a richly anointed offering.

GMLA continues to dream of a broader, deeper global mission, breaking the barriers of language and culture through creative literary and artistic ministry. With over 30 members walking this path together, we devote ourselves daily to the sacred labor of creation. As we look to the future, we recognize the need for mission-minded members with spiritual depth and professional excellence. This journey requires humility, authenticity, and spiritual unity.

We earnestly invite your prayers and financial support—whether direct or indirect—as we press on toward the vision God has entrusted to us.

간증

다시 걷는 길, 아데니움

이신헌

"여보… 눈 좀 떠요… 여보!"
 그날 아침은 평소와 다름없이 시작되었다. 성경을 펼쳐 묵상하던 손끝이 이상하게 떨릴 때까지만 해도, 나는 단순한 피로려니 생각했다. 가끔 소화가 안되고 손발에 힘이 풀렸지만 대수롭지 않게 여겼다. 그날 밤, 나는 의자에서 떨어져 내렸고, 오른쪽 팔과 다리는 내 것이 아닌 듯 무거워졌다.
 급히 달려온 사위가 떨리는 손으로 119에 전화를 걸었고, 나는 흐릿한 시야 너머로 아내가 눈물로 "제발… 살려 주세요"라며 부르짖는 모습을 보았다. 사이렌 소리, 병원 천장의 형광등, 그리고 점점 멀어져 가는 의식 속에서, 내가 마지막으로 들은 말은 의사의 냉정한 한마디였다.
 "뇌경색입니다. 언어와 운동 기능에 심각한 손상이 있습니다."
 응급실로 들어가면서 나는 길고 긴 수렁같은 음습하고 황량한 곳으로 빠져 오래 오래 멀고 먼 길을 헤매었다. 수만 개의 어두운 손들이 나를 잡아끄는 것 같았다. 억만 톤 흑암의 세포가 나를 잡아 삼키는 듯 했다.

 막막한 사막 같은 길이 가로막았다. 가방 하나 들고 먼 길을 떠났다. 젊었을 때의 꿈, 영어로 설교하고 싶은 꿈, 현지의 목회자들에게 영어로 신학을 가르치고, 내 목회 경험을 전하고 싶은 꿈, 그 꿈을 찾기 위해 국내 안정되고 남들이 부러워하는 목회자의 자리를 넘기고 아내와 함께 마닐라행 비행기에 몸을 실었다.

이신헌 목사는 목포 제일교회 목회를 은퇴 후 필리핀에서 8년간 시니어 선교사 사역을 하던 중, 코로나로 귀국, 뇌경색으로 쓰러져 사막과 같은 힘든 투쟁과 재활의 시간 4년을 극복하고 다시 일어나 주님 나라 위해 열심히 사역 중입니다.

The Road Walked Again, Adenium

Rev. Shinheon Lee

"My dear... open your eyes... please, open your eyes…"

That morning began no differently than others. My fingers trembled oddly as I opened the Bible for meditation, but I dismissed it as mere fatigue. Occasional indigestion, the weakness in my limbs—I had brushed them aside. But that night, I fell from my chair, and my right arm and leg turned heavy, as if they no longer belonged to me. My son-in-law, trembling, dialed 911. Through the haze in my vision, I saw my wife crying out, "Please… please save him…" Her voice, soaked in tears, echoed in the distance. Sirens wailed. The fluorescent lights on the hospital ceiling blurred above me, and consciousness began to fade. The last voice I heard was cold and sharp.

"Stroke. Severe damage to language and motor function."
As I was wheeled into the ER, I felt myself slipping into a deep, endless abyss—a cold and desolate wilderness. It was as if ten thousand dark hands pulled me downward, as if the weight of a billion shadows sought to swallow me whole.

A pathless desert lay before me. Carrying nothing but a single bag, I had once set out on a long journey. I left behind the comfort and respect of pastoral ministry in Korea, chasing an old dream—to preach in English, to teach theology to local pastors, to pass on my ministry experience. With my wife by my side, I boarded a plane to Manila, believing there was still purpose ahead.

간
증

" 여보 당신은 잘 할 수 있을 거에요. 고등학교 시절부터 배운 영어 발음은 최고에요. 조금만 더 애쓰시면 설교도 잘 할 수 있을 거에요!"

늘 나를 응원하는 소중한 아내의 목소리에 힘을 얻어 필리핀 작은 도시 카인타에 도착하고 얼마 지나지 않아 주일에 영어 설교를 준비하게 되었다. 원고를 죄다 외웠다. 눈감고도 할 수 있도록 성구를 외우고, 모든 글자를 외울 때까지 잠을 자지 않고 밤을 새웠다.

얼마 지나 신학교에서 영어로 강의를 맡게 되었다. 온몸을 땀으로 적시는 강의를 하면서 나는 꿈에 그리던 그때를 떠올렸다. 사막에도 길이 있음을, 길을 여시는 이는 주님이심을 깨달았다. 칠 년여 동안 필리핀에서 시니어 선교사역을 하는 사이사이 건강점검을 위해 국내를 오가며 진단을 받곤 했다. 내 몸이 쇠약함을 느낄 때마다, 시니어 선교사로서의 사역이 힘에 부칠 때마다 늘 말씀을 붙잡곤 했다.

"내가 사망의 음침한 골짜기로 다닐지라도 해를 두려워하지 않을 것은 주께서 나와 함께 하심이라 주의 지팡이와 막대기가 나를 안위하시나이다"

"You can do it, my love. Your English pronunciation—ever since high school—has always been the best. Just a little more effort, and you'll preach beautifully."

It was her voice—my beloved wife, always my strongest encourager—that breathed life into my weary heart. Not long after arriving in Cainta, a small city in the Philippines, I was asked to prepare an English sermon for Sunday worship.
I memorized every word. I stayed up all night, refusing to sleep until I could recite the Scriptures with my eyes closed, until each syllable was etched into my mind like a prayer.

Soon after, I was invited to teach theology in English at a seminary. My body drenched in sweat with every lecture, I remembered the dream I had once cradled in my heart. Yes, even in the desert, there is a path. And it is the Lord who opens the way.
Throughout the seven years I served as a senior missionary in the Philippines, I traveled back and forth to Korea for medical checkups. Every time my body grew weak, every time the burden of ministry felt too great for me to bear, I clung to the Word—my only anchor in the dry and weary land.

"**Even though I walk through the valley of the shadow of death, I will fear no evil, for You are with me; Your rod and Your staff, they comfort me.**"

간증

 2019년, 코로나가 전 세계를 덮쳐서 모든 공항이 마비되기 불과 1주 전, 아내와 나는 정기 건강 검진을 위해 한국으로 향하는 비행기에 몸을 실었다. 어쩌면 영원히 다시 돌아올 수 없는 비행기인지도 모르고, 푸르른 하늘을 쳐다보며 더 많은 상상과 꿈의 세계로 들어갔다. 멀지 않아 내게 닥쳐올 거대한 죽음의 산이 있다는 것도 모른 채 설레임으로 인천 공항에 발을 내렸다.

 2021, 2월 코로나 뉴스로 온 땅이 불안과 염려로 차 있던 당시, 국내에 돌아와 건강 검진을 받고 몸을 추스르던 나는 몸에 이상 증세가 옴을 감지하게 되었다. 추운 겨울, 소화 장애가 늘 일어나 식후에 걷기를 하였다. 매일 아침 식사 후, 점심 식사 후 저녁까지 하루에 3회 30분씩 90분을 걸었다. 눈이 올 때는 지하 주차장을 사용하였다. 그런 중에 가끔 소화 장애가 오고 구토를 하였다. 이상하게 생각하지 않고 열심히 걷기를 하였다.

 그런데 밤 중에 오른 쪽 다리에 힘이 빠졌다. 밤 2 시경, 당황하였지만 잠을 청했는데 잠시 후 오른 손, 오른 다리가 풀려서 아내를 불렀다. 아내가 사위에게 급히 전화를 하였다. 119가 와서 싣고 가까운 한국병원으로 갔다. 병원 응급실의 조처가 신속하지 못했다. 그러나 병원에서 사진을 찍은 후에도 병 상태를 정확하게 말해주지 못하고, 담당 의사가 우왕좌왕 하였다.

In 2019, just one week before the global pandemic shut down every airport in the world, my wife and I boarded a plane bound for Korea for our routine health checkups. We did not know—it could have been a flight from which we would never return. As we looked up at the clear blue sky, our hearts were filled with dreams and imagination, unaware that a towering mountain of death was quietly approaching.

By February 2021, the world was suffocating in fear, gripped by the daily onslaught of COVID news. Back in Korea, while recovering and undergoing medical tests, I began to sense that something was wrong in my body. That bitter winter, indigestion became a constant companion. I began walking after every meal—thirty minutes in the morning, afternoon, and evening, totaling ninety minutes each day. When snow fell, I walked alone in the dim underground parking garage. Even when I vomited or suffered discomfort, I pushed on, thinking little of it—just walking, walking, walking.

Then, one night, I felt the strength in my right leg fade. It was around 2 a.m. I was alarmed, but I tried to sleep it off. Soon after, my right hand and leg went limp. I called out to my wife in fear. She quickly contacted our son-in-law, and before long, the paramedics arrived and rushed me to a nearby hospital. The emergency response was sluggish. Even after taking scans, the doctors couldn't clearly explain my condition. The attending physician was confused and unprepared.

간증

　　뇌경색이 나를 강타했다. 응급실로 들어가며 나는 아내를 향해 계속 말했다
　　" 미안해 여보 미안해 미안해 여보!"

　　오랜 시간 후에 반쯤 마비된 몸으로 깨어났다. 말은 입술에 맴돌 뿐 나오지 않았고, 기도하던 손은 성경 한 장 넘기기조차 버거웠다. 성경을 읽지도, 말씀을 전하지도 못하는 선교사라니. 그것은 날개 없는 새처럼, 숨 쉴 수 없는 사명자처럼 느껴졌다. 재활 병동의 창문은 낮게 깔린 구름처럼 우울했고, 낮에는 통증이, 밤에는 고독이 찾아왔다.

　　"왜 나입니까, 주님…" 속으로만 웅얼이던 그 질문은 눈물로도 씻을 수 없는 깊은 통곡이 되었다. 아내는 매일 새벽 내 손을 잡고 기도했다. 입도 제대로 못 여는 나를 대신해 그녀는 나 대신 시편 23편을 읽어 주었고, 매끼 식사를 떠먹여 주며 웃어 주었다. 어느 날 그녀는 조용히 속삭였다.
　　"여보, 당신은 아직 끝나지 않았어요. 하나님께서 일하시고 계세요. 나는 매일, 당신이 다시 말씀을 전하는 모습을 그리며 기도해요."
　　그 말은 사막에서 피어나는 꽃처럼 내 마음에 머물렀다.

　　한국병원에서 4개월 입원 치료 중 다시 목포의 원광 한의원에서 2개월 입원치료를 받고 3년 5개월 동안 외래치료를 받았다. 그 후 뇌 상태를 좀 더 깊이 관찰하기 위하여 서울 세브란스 병원으로 옮겼다. 정밀한 사진을 찍고, 치료 약도 확인하고 싶었다.

A stroke struck me like a storm. While I went to ER, I repeated " I am sorry Honey sorry sorry !" After long hours, I awoke to a body half-paralyzed. Words danced on my lips but could not form; the hands once lifted in prayer could not even turn a single page of the Bible. A missionary who can not read the Word, who cannot preach—what worth was I now? I felt like a bird without wings, like a servant of God gasping for breath, buried under the silence. The windows of the rehabilitation ward hung low with clouds of sorrow. Pain visited me by day, and loneliness wrapped around me at night.

"Why me, Lord…?" The words I could not voice churned within, until they spilled out in tears I could not stop. My wife held my hand every dawn and prayed. For the mouth that could no longer speak, she read Psalm 23 aloud. She fed me each meal with a gentle smile and whispered softly one day:
"My love, this is not the end. God is still working.
Every day, I pray to see you preach again."
That whisper took root in my heart like a flower blooming in the desert.

I stayed four months in the Korean hospital, then moved to Mokpo to continue inpatient treatment for another two months at the Wonkwang Korean Medicine Clinic. Outpatient care followed for three years and five months. Later, I was transferred to Severance Hospital in Seoul for deeper evaluation of my brain condition— to capture more precise images and confirm the right course of medication.

그런 과정 속에서 가장 소중하고 없어서는 안 될 사랑하는 아내 박효영 사모의 헌신과 뜨거운 기도와 사랑으로 힘겨운 재활을 하게 되었다. 재활은 생각보다 훨씬 더디고 고통스러웠다. 무엇보다 나는 말하는 것을 회복하기 위해 가장 많은 노력을 기울였다. 작은 발음 하나를 뱉기 위해 혀를 깨물고, 숟가락을 들기까지 한 달이 걸렸다. 어느 날, 나는 내 이름 석 자를 쓰는 데 성공했고, 아내는 그걸 보며 조용히 눈물을 닦았다. 그날부터였다. 내 회복은 작지만 분명한 속도로 진행되었다.

이전처럼 유창하게 설교하지는 못했지만, 나는 한 문장씩 다시 말씀을 읽기 시작했다. 나는 전에 그리던 그림을 그리기 위해 떨리는 손을 집중하며 수묵화를 그려나갔다. 아마도 수백 번 버리고 또 버리며 손끝 하나에 힘을 주어 집중하며 심혈을 기울였다. 언젠가 내 그림이 누군가 힘을 잃고 눈물 흘리는 이의 방에 걸려 힘내라고 위로를 건네줄 것을 믿으며!

**"내 영혼을 소생시키시고 자기 이름을 위하여
　　　의의 길로 인도 하시는도다"**

사 년 뒤 목회자 수련회에서 초청하여 강단에 섰다. 거의 천 오백 여일 만에 나는 매일 꿈에 그리던 강단에 다시 서게 되었다. 아내가 나를 보며 염려 반 믿음 반, 그러나 반드시 승리하리라는 믿음의 눈으로 내게 말해 왔다.

In the midst of it all, it was the unwavering love, fervent prayers, and sacrificial devotion of my beloved wife, Pastor Park Hyo-Young, that carried me through the darkest valleys of recovery. Rehabilitation was far slower and more painful than I had imagined. Above all, I poured everything into regaining my ability to speak. To form even the smallest sound, I bit down on my tongue; it took an entire month before I could lift a spoon to my mouth. Then one day, I managed to write my own name—just three simple characters. My wife quietly wiped her tears as she watched. From that day forward, my recovery began—slow, but sure, like the first drip of rain in a long drought.

I could no longer preach with the same fluency as before, but I began to read the Word again—one sentence at a time. And I returned to the brush, trembling hand focused on strokes of ink and hope. Hundreds of times I crumpled my work, tried again, concentrating every fiber of strength into each movement. I believed—no, I knew—that someday, one of my paintings would hang in a room where someone sits in sorrow, and whisper to them: Do not give up.

"He restores my soul; He leads me in paths of righteousness for His name's sake."

Four years later, I was invited to speak at a pastors' retreat. After nearly 1,500 days, I stood once more at the pulpit I had dreamed of daily. My wife looked at me—part fear, part faith—but her eyes declared with certainty: You will overcome. You will stand victorious.

온몸과 다리와 손이 떨려오고 말할 자신도 없었지만 호흡을 가다듬고 마이크 앞에서 천천히, 그러나 확실하게 첫 마디를 꺼냈다.
"여러분, 쓰러졌던 그 자리가 하나님이 저를 다시 세우신 자리였습니다."

아내는 조용히 뒤에서 손을 모은 채 울고 있었다. 나는 안다. 그녀의 기도와 눈물, 헌신 없이는 이 자리에 설 수 없었다는 것을. 사람들은 내 회복을 기적이라 불렀지만, 나는 안다. 그것은 '믿음'이 걸은 길이었다. 고통 속에서도 다시 걷는 그 길. 사막의 길에도 하나님의 능력의 손길이 닿고 있음을, 사막 메마른 곳에도 장미꽃보다 고운 꽃이 피어난다는 것을!

나는 매일 셀레임으로 "아데니움"이란 단어를 써 본다. 아데니움을 주제로 그림을 그린다. 사막의 장미꽃! 내 지난 오 년여 길고 긴 죽음의 사막길에 포기하면 안 된다고 밤마다 꿈속에서 일깨워 주며 힘을 주던 아데니움, 밤마다 사막에서 들려오는 "아데니움" 노래를 부르며 불편한 몸을 움직여 춤을 춰 본다. 내게 주어진 남은 생이 다하는 날까지, 더 멀리, 더 높이, 더 깊이 하나님 아버지의 사랑과 부활을 전하기 위해!

Though my whole body trembled—my legs, my hands—and I had no confidence to speak, I steadied my breath. And standing before the microphone, I slowly, yet surely, spoke the first words:

"Friends, the very place where I fell… is the place where God chose to raise me up again."

Behind me, my wife stood quietly, hands clasped in prayer, tears silently falling. I knew. Without her prayers, her tears, and her unwavering devotion—I would not be standing here today. People called it a miracle—this recovery of mine. But I knew. It was the path walked by faith. A path walked through pain. Even in the desert, the hand of God's power reaches out. Even in barren lands, flowers more beautiful than roses can bloom.

Every day, with trembling hope, I write the word: Adenium.

I paint with Adenium as my theme—the desert rose. It is the very flower that whispered to me night after night through the long, deathly desert road of the past five years, Don't give up. Each night, I dream of the desert singing the word Adenium. And I try to move this uncomfortable body—to dance, even if clumsily—singing along with the voice of the desert. And until the day my remaining breath is spent,

I will go farther, rise higher, and go deeper—

To proclaim the Father's love and the power of the Resurrection.

고자질

고승희

고요한 밤, 침묵 속에 숨어있던 작은 목소리가 들려와
잊고 싶었던 과거의 조각들, 숨기고 싶었던 파편들,
어둠 속에서 하나둘씩 모습을 드러내고 있어 무서워

날카로운 송곳니가 내 마음의 벽을 긁어내고, 기억의
낡은 서랍을 삐그덕덕 열어젖히고 있어 후회의 그림자,
죄책감의 무게가 어깨를 짓누르면 어떡해 난!

외면하고 싶던 진실들 속삭이며 나를 괴롭혀 와
수천 겹 고자질은 멈추지 않아. 밤새도록 내 약점을
들춰내며 너야 너 모든 게 너 때문이야 알곤 있어?

밀물처럼 새벽이 밀려와 무서워 날 좀 찾아 줘
숨을 곳이 없어 동녘으로 빛이 점점 다가와
날 좀 제발, 니 손짓이라도 보여줘 숨쉬고 싶어 제발

고승희 선교사는 중국에서 20년동안 의료사역 후, 현재 필리핀에서 GO Clinic을 운영하며 신학교에서 사역하고 있다. 글로벌선교문학회 회원으로 활동 중이다.

Tattletale

by Ko Seung-hee

In the quiet night, a soft voice creeps,
Whispers from the past, fragments I tried to keep.
Things I wanted to forget, pieces I tried to hide,
They show up one by one in the dark, and I can't deny.

Sharp fangs scrape the walls of my mind,
Opening old drawers, memories left behind.
The shadow of regret, the weight of guilt,
Pressing on my shoulders, how am I supposed to deal?

Truths I tried to avoid, they whisper in my ear,
Thousand layers of tattling, they won't disappear.
All night, pulling at my weaknesses, exposing my flaw,
It's you, it's you, everything's your fault, do you see it, or not?

Like the tide, the dawn creeps in,
I'm scared, someone, please find me again.
No place to hide, the light's creeping near,
Show me your hand, I just want to breathe, I fear.

생명의 길, 혈관의 노래

고승희

고요한 새벽, 손목 안쪽의 미세한 맥박을 느낀다.
쿵, 쿵. 규칙적인 리듬에 맞춰 내 몸 안의 작은 강물이
흐르고 있음을 깨닫는다. 그 강물의 이름은 혈관,
생명의 에너지를 실어 나르는 신비로운 통로다.

어린 시절, 혈관은 그저 빨간색과 파란색의 가는 선으로만
여겼다. 하지만 성장하고 몸의 구조를 배우면서 혈관의
놀라운 역할들을 알게 되었다. 혈관은 심장에서 뿜어져
나온 혈액을 온몸 구석구석으로 전달하고, 세포에서 발생
한 노폐물을 다시 심장으로 운반한다. 마치 도시의 복잡한
도로망처럼, 혈관은 우리 몸의 모든 곳을 연결하며 생명
유지에 필수적인 역할을 수행한다.

혈관은 때로는 굵고 강인한 모습으로, 때로는 가늘고
섬세한 모습으로 우리 몸속을 누빈다. 굵은 동맥은
심장의 힘찬 박동을 온몸으로 전달하고, 가느다란
모세혈관은 세포 하나하나에 필요한 산소와 영양분을
공급한다. 마치 숙련된 택배 기사처럼, 혈관은 필요한
물자를 정확하게 전달하고 불필요한 노폐물을 신속
하게 처리한다.

The Path of Life, the Song of Blood Vessels
by Ko Seung-hee

In the quiet dawn, I feel the tiny pulse on the inside of my wrist. Thump, thump. In rhythm, I realize that a small river flows within my body. This river is called blood vessels, a mysterious path carrying the energy of life.

As a child, I thought blood vessels were just thin red and blue lines. But as I grew and learned about the body's structure, I discovered the amazing roles of blood vessels. They carry the blood pumped from the heart to every part of the body, and bring back waste products from the cells to the heart. Like a complex network of roads in a city, blood vessels connect all parts of our body and play an essential role in keeping us alive.

Blood vessels sometimes appear thick and strong, and other times, they are thin and delicate. Thick arteries carry the strong beats of the heart to the entire body, while tiny capillaries supply oxygen and nutrients to each cell. Like a skilled delivery person, blood vessels accurately deliver what is needed and quickly remove waste.

하지만 현대 사회의 혈관은 끊임없이 위협받고 있다. 고지방, 고콜레스테롤 식단, 운동 부족, 스트레스 등은 혈관을 좁아지게 하고 막히게 한다. 마치 녹슨 파이프처럼, 혈관은 점점 그 기능을 잃어간다. 혈관 건강이 악화되면 고혈압, 동맥경화, 심근경색, 뇌졸중 등 심각한 질환으로 이어질 수 있다.

나는 혈관에게 감사한 마음을 전한다. 그동안 너무 소홀하게 대했던 것은 아닌지, 너무 많은 부담을 주었던 것은 아닌지 반성한다. 이제부터라도 혈관의 목소리에 귀 기울이고, 혈관 건강을 위해 노력하기로 다짐한다. 건강한 식습관을 유지하고, 꾸준한 운동을 통해 혈관을 튼튼하게 만들 것이다. 또한, 스트레스를 현명하게 관리하고, 충분한 휴식을 취하며 혈관에게 편안한 환경을 제공할 것이다.

혈관은 우리 몸의 생명선이자, 건강의 바로미터다. 혈관 건강은 곧 우리 삶의 질과 직결된다. 생명의 길, 혈관의 노래에 귀 기울이며, 앞으로도 함께 건강한 삶을 만들어 나가기를 소망한다.

However, in modern society, blood vessels are constantly under threat. Diets high in fat and cholesterol, lack of exercise, and stress cause blood vessels to narrow and become blocked. Like rusted pipes, blood vessels gradually lose their function. When blood vessel health worsens, it can lead to serious conditions like high blood pressure, arteriosclerosis, heart attacks, and strokes.

I express my gratitude to my blood vessels. I reflect on whether I've neglected them too much, whether I've given them too much burden. From now on, I promise to listen to their voice, and to take care of my blood vessel health. I will maintain a healthy diet, exercise regularly to strengthen my blood vessels, manage stress wisely, and provide a comfortable environment by getting enough rest.

Blood vessels are the lifeline of our body and a barometer of our health. The health of our blood vessels directly affects the quality of our life. By listening to the song of blood vessels, I hope to continue building a healthy life together.

나의 몸, 성스러운 선교지
고승희

나는 매일 아침, 나의 몸이라는 미지의 대륙으로 떠나는 선교사다. 낡고 허름한 지도를 손에 쥐고, 삐걱거리는 나침반에 의지한 채, 나는 내 몸 구석구석을 탐험한다. 이곳은 아직 문명의 손길이 닿지 않은 미개척지와 같다. 곳곳에 숨겨진 비밀과 놀라운 생명력에 나는 매번 감탄한다.

나의 선교는 숭고한 의식을 동반한다. 굳어버린 관절에 따뜻한 온기를 불어넣고, 뭉친 근육을 부드럽게 풀어준다. 낡은 세포들은 새로운 활력을 얻고, 지친 장기들은 평온을 되찾는다. 나는 내 몸의 찬양을 듣는다. 뼈마디가 부딪히는 소리, 심장이 고동치는 소리, 폐가 숨 쉬는 소리. 이 모든 소리는 생명의 교향곡이다.

그러나 나의 선교는 순탄치만은 않다. 때로는 고통이라는 이름의 거센 폭풍우가 몰아치고, 때로는 질병이라는 이름의 사악한 마녀가 나타난다. 그럴 때마다 나는 더욱 굳건히 마음을 다잡는다. 고통은 내 몸의 외침이다. 질병은 내 몸의 시험이다. 나는 그들의 목소리에 귀 기울이고, 그들의 시련을 극복하기 위해 최선을 다한다.

My Body, the Sacred Mission Field

by Ko Seung-hee

Every morning, I become a missionary embarking on a journey to the unknown continent of my body. With an old, tattered map in hand, and relying on a creaky compass, I explore every corner of my body. This place is like an uncharted land, untouched by civilization. I marvel at the hidden secrets and the remarkable vitality in every part.

My mission is accompanied by sacred rituals. I breathe warmth into stiff joints and gently loosen tight muscles. Old cells are revitalized, and weary organs regain peace. I listen to the praises of my body. The sound of bones clicking, the beating of my heart, the breath of my lungs— these are the symphonies of life.

However, my mission is not always easy. Sometimes, a fierce storm named pain strikes, and at times, an evil witch called illness appears. In those moments, I strengthen my resolve. Pain is the cry of my body. Illness is the test of my body. I listen to their voices, and I do my best to overcome their trials.

나의 선교는 봉사와 헌신을 요구한다. 때로는 달콤한
유혹을 뿌리쳐야 하고, 때로는 불편한 진실과 마주해야
한다. 하지만 나는 멈추지 않는다. 내 몸은 나의 성전이자
나의 책임이기 때문이다. 나는 내 몸을 사랑하고 존중하며,
내 몸의 건강과 행복을 위해 끊임없이 노력한다.

나의 선교는 아직 끝나지 않았다. 내 몸이라는 대륙은
여전히 탐험할 곳이 많다. 나는 매일 새로운 발걸음
을 내딛고, 새로운 지도를 그려나간다. 내 몸의 신비를
밝혀내고, 내 몸의 잠재력을 일깨우는 것, 그것이 바로
나의 사명이다.

나는 내 몸을 선교한다. 내 몸은 나의 가장 소중한
선교지이기 때문이다.

My mission requires service and dedication. At times, I must resist the sweet temptations, and at other times, face uncomfortable truths. But I do not stop, for my body is my temple and my responsibility. I love and respect my body, and I constantly strive for its health and happiness.

My mission is not yet complete. The continent of my body still holds many uncharted territories. Each day, I take a new step and draw a new map. Uncovering the mysteries of my body, awakening its potential—this is my mission.

I mission to my body, for my body is my most cherished mission field.

십자가. 2

고정옥

십자가로 나는 다시 태어났네.
꽁꽁 얼어 붙었던 흙 덩어리,
영혼의 대지에 새 생명 움트었네.

십자가로 나는 당신을 만났네.
향방 없는 한 마리의 새,
홀로 허공을 헤메일 때
내간 만난 이정표.
또 삶에 길잡이가 되었네.

십자가 지신 당신만을 자랑하네.
아름다운 샤론의 꽃,
당신의 신부 되어.
다시 오실 당신을 노래하네.

고정옥 선교사는 국내에서 17년 사역자로 섬기다. 2014년 선교사로 필리핀에 파송된 이래 바라스 이레 교회, 랑까안 주안교회를 섬기며, 글로벌선교문학회 회원, 워십댄스 팀 에이레네 리더로 활동 중이다.

The Cross. 2
by Go Jung-ok

Through the cross, I was born again.
The earth, once frozen tight,
Now bears new life,
sprouting on the soil of my soul.

Through the cross, I met You.
A bird with no direction,
Wandering alone through the air,
I found the signpost of my heart.
Once again, You became my guide in life.

Only You, who bore the cross, I boast of.
The beautiful flower of Sharon,
I became Your bride,
And I sing of Your return, O Lord.

로뎀나무 아래에서

고정옥

갈멜산에 그분을 잊었다 죽음의 고비에서... 나는 열심이 특심이고 믿음이 자랑인 사람이였다. 그러나 승리의 위풍당당함도 위기 순간엔 커다란 두려움으로 옷 입었다. 떡 한 쪽으로 나의 자존심까지 땅에 떨어졌다. 사렙다 가난한 과부에게 구걸하기 보다는 차라리 그릿 시냇가 까마귀가 더 나았다.

주체 할 수 없이 거대한 이세벨에 쫓겨 달리고 또 달렸는데 눈 떠보니 광야였다. 또 다시 지친 몸을 끌고 간 곳은 사막, 안전지대를 찾아 몇 마일을 걷고 걸었는데도 황량한 광야에 로뎀나무만 있다. 허기진 두려움과 갈라진 목마름으로 꺼져가는 심지

가장 소중한 것을 잃은 늑대처럼 고개를 들어 힘껏 반항했다. 차라리 생명을 거두어 달라고 그편이 나을꺼라고... 그렇게 한바탕 하늘을 노려보다가 로뎀나무 아래서 깊은 잠에 취했다

뜨거운 광야 바람이 침묵으로 다가왔다. 그분의 사랑의 편지, 떡과 물, 눈물 방울을 본다. 사막의 추운 밤 따뜻한 달빛의 세레나데로 영혼을 감싸준다. 영롱한 아침 이슬이 아무 말 없이 먼지에 쌓인 얼굴을 감싸주며 눈물을 닦아준다 '괜찮아 실패가 아니라, 실현이란다 '

Beneath the Broom Tree
by Ko Jeong-ok

I forgot Him on Mount Carmel— Even on the edge of death, I, who once burned with zeal, Who wore faith like a crown, Stood trembling As triumph turned to terror. With one crust of bread, My pride crumbled into dust. Better the ravens at Cherith Than begging from a widow in Zarephath.

Fleeing— Chased by the towering shadow of Jezebel, I ran, and ran, Until my eyes opened to a wilderness that had no end. Dragging my weariness, I walked for miles through sand and silence, Hoping for shelter, Finding only a broom tree In the vast, unbroken desert.

My thirst cracked my lips, Fear gnawed at my hunger, And the flame of hope Dwindled to a flickering thread. Like a wolf that has lost its cub, I raised my head and roared—
"Take my life! Better death than this hollow breath!"
And with clenched fists I stared down the sky, Then collapsed beneath the tree, Into sleep.

The heat of the desert Spoke in hushes, Carrying the whisper of His love— Bread. Water. Tears. And in the cold of the night, Moonlight wrapped around my soul Like a lullaby, And in the silence of dawn, The glistening dew Wiped the dust from my face— Wiped away my tears.
"It's not failure," "It's fulfillment."

또 다시 아버지의 밥상, 떡과 물, 하늘의 숨결이 사랑의 노래로 구름 위를 걷게 한다. 아버지가 차려주신 두 번째 광야 밥상을 먹고도 허기짐에 허덕인다. 또 다시 아버지가 따뜻하게 바람의 손길로 어루만지신다.

'잘했어 실패가 아니라 실현이야 '

나의 찢긴 살 어루만지시어 회복시키시며 아버지의 손길로 나의 상처에 핏 방울로 수혈해 주신다

그러나 세 번째 다시 세상이란 깜깜한 동굴에 안주한다. 나 조차도 포기한 나를 포기하지 않는 아버지, 한심한 못난이라 치부한 나에게 호통치지 않고 인자한 아버지의 햇볕으로 동굴속 숨어 있는 내게 말한다.

"괜찮아 다시 힘을 얻자 엘리사를 세우는 사명, 다음 세대를 세우는 사명 네게 있단다" 아버지의 손을 잡고 나의 안주의 그물을 벗고 동굴에서 사명의 세상으로 나온다.

이제 나의 겉옷은 더 이상 구질구질한 누더기가 아니라 능력의 겉옷이다. 엘리사를 세울 사명, 세상에 선한 영향력을 발휘할 주님의 제자를 세우는 일, 내가 할 나머지 일이라고. 지나가는 바람에게 속삭인다.

'로뎀나무 그늘은 실패의 자리가 아닌 도약을 위한 쉼이였다'. 라고

Once Again, the Father's Table Once again, The Father lays the table— Bread and water, The breath of heaven— A song of love That lets me walk upon the clouds. And yet⋯ Even after the second meal in the wilderness, I hunger still. I stumble still. But once more, The Father reaches out, Warm wind upon my wounds.

"Well done. It wasn't failure—it was formation."

He touches my torn flesh, Heals what is broken, Infuses His very blood Into my wounds With the kindness of His hand.

Still— A third time, I retreat again Into the cave called "World,"

Dark and safe. Even I have given up on me. But not the Father. He does not scold, He does not shame. He comes, Gentle sunlight slipping through the cracks, And speaks into my hiding:

"It's alright. Let's rise again. You have a calling—To raise Elisha, To raise the next generation."

I take His hand. I tear the net of my false comfort. I step out of the cave And into the world of mission.

Now my outer cloak is no longer ragged with regret— It is a mantle of power. A mission remains: To raise Elisha, To shape disciples Who will bear God's light Into the shadows of the earth.

And I whisper to the passing wind:

"The shade of the broom tree Was never failure— It was the rest before the rise."

엄마는 무척 꽃을 좋아합니다
고정옥

    오월의 어느 날, 봄볕이 포근히 스며든 신촌 거리. 병원에 가는 길, 상점 안엔 초록빛 화장품, 보라빛 원피스, 핑크빛 속옷들이 눈을 사로잡고, 가로수 그늘아래 작은 꽃들이 활짝 피어 있었습니다. 지나는 바람엔 꽃내음이 실려 와 봄의 편지를 건네주었고, 내 마음엔 어느새 장미빛 미소가 피어났습니다. 꽃을 보고 있으니, 문득 떠오른 얼굴-엄마였습니다.

    엄마도 참 꽃을 좋아하셨지요. 그날 저는 엄마를 떠올리며 파란빛이 도는 하얀 장미를 바구니에 담았습니다. 팔순을 넘긴 엄마께 드리자, 연분홍빛 수국처럼 환히 웃으셨습니다. 그러나 그 웃음 뒤엔, 삶의 풍파를 그대로 새긴 얼굴, 눈물과 바람이 지나간 자국이 하나하나 남아 있었습니다.

    엄마의 고향은 전남 구례, 그중에서도 더 깊은 산골 마을, 간전면 대촌리입니다. 2남 3녀 중 맏딸로 태어난 엄마는 총명하셨고, 공부도 잘하셨습니다. 하지만 가난한 두메산골, 소꼴을 먹이고, 밤을 줍고, 논밭을 거드는 게 일상이었습니다.

Mother Truly Loved Flowers
by Ko Jung-ok

One gentle day in May, sunlight softly draped the streets of Sinchon. On my way to the hospital, shop windows bloomed with green-toned cosmetics, lilac dresses, and tender pink undergarments. Beneath the trees lining the sidewalk, tiny blossoms peeked out from flowerpots, while the breeze carried the sweet scent of spring— a letter from the season itself, whispering warmth into my heart. And just like that, a soft smile—like a blooming rose—touched my face. Looking at the flowers, one face suddenly came to mind: Mother.

She loved flowers dearly. Thinking of her that day, I placed a white rose tinged with blue into a basket. When I offered it to her, now well into her eighties, she smiled—bright as a blush-pink hydrangea. But behind that radiant smile was a face carved by the years— etched by hardship, weathered by tears and winds that had passed.

Mother was born in a remote mountain village—Dacchon-ri in Ganjun-myeon, deep within Gurye, South Jeolla Province. The eldest of five children, she was bright and gifted in her studies. Yet life in the countryside was harsh. Feeding the cows, gathering chestnuts, helping in the fields—such was her childhood, rooted in labor and resilience.

호롱불 아래 책을 펼치면, "기름 아깝다"며 호통치시던 할아버지 때문에 땅바닥에 나뭇가지로 수학 문제를 풀어야 했고, 남의 밭 조롱박에 한자를 새겨 넣었다가 오히려 글솜씨 좋다는 칭찬을 받았답니다. 그토록 공부를 좋아했지만, "여자에게 공부는 사치"라는 외할아버지의 말에 중학교 진학 대신 바느질과 자수를 배워야 했습니다.

그렇게 스무 살, 꽃 같은 나이에 엄마는 섬진강을 나룻배로 건너 구례읍의 한 찻집에서 아버지와 맞선을 보고 결혼했습니다. 늦둥이셨던 아버지는 조실부모 후, 큰형님 밑에서 힘겹게 살아오신 분이었고 엄마의 신혼은 그 형님의 집 사랑방에서 시작되었습니다.

그 집엔 이미 7남매의 조카들이 있었고, 엄마는 자연스럽게 모든 살림을 맡게 되셨습니다. 손 시린 겨울날, 얼음을 깨고 손빨래를 하시며 그 많은 식구의 밥과 옷, 밭일까지 감당하셨습니다. 그 모든 시간을 엄마는 불평 없이, 지혜와 사랑으로 지나오셨습니다. 그리고 1남 5녀의 자녀와 5남 2녀의 조카들을 한 사람 한 사람 정성껏 길러내셨습니다.

At night, she would open her books under the glow of a small oil lamp— only to be scolded by her grandfather:
"Don't waste the oil!" So she took to solving math problems on the dirt floor with a twig. She once carved Chinese characters into the gourds hanging in a neighbor's field, and rather than being punished, she was praised—for the beauty of her script. She loved studying with all her heart, but in her grandfather's stern view, education was a luxury for girls.

And so, at the tender age of twenty, in full bloom like a spring flower, Mother crossed the Seomjin River by ferryand met my father in a small teahouse in Gurye-eup. He was the youngest son of his family, orphaned at two, raised by his much older brother through hardship and toil. Their newlywed life began in the sarangbang—a guest room—of that brother's home.

There were already seven children in the household, and Mother, without question, took charge of all the chores. On freezing winter days, she broke through ice to hand-wash laundry, prepared meals for the many mouths, stitched clothes, and worked the fields. Through it all, she never complained. With grace and quiet strength, she carried her days with wisdom and love. She raised not only her own six children—one son and five daughters— but also cared devotedly for her husband's nieces and nephews, five boys and two girls, as if each were her own.

동인작가 글

    부모는, 신이 보내신 자식이라는 나무를 가꾸는 정원사라고 합니다. 엄마와 아버지의 사랑이 깃든 정원에서 자란 우리는 지금 각자의 삶에서 향기로운 꽃으로 피어 있습니다.

    이제 내 아들과 딸도 어느새 스무 살 청년이 되었습니다. 아직 어린 것 같은 이 아이들을 보며, 그보다 훨씬 어린 나이에 인생의 무게를 지고 가정을 일구어 가신 엄마의 모습이 더욱 깊은 존경으로 다가옵니다. 나는 우리 아이들에게 어떤 씨앗을 심고 있을까요?

    나는 하늘 아버지께서 맡기신 자녀들의 정원사입니다. 지혜의 양분, 사랑의 햇볕, 정성의 물을 주며 탐스러운 꽃으로 피어나도록 돕는, 그런 정원사 말입니다. 이제는 품안의 자식들이 또다시 부모가 되어 세상의 바람을 맞으며 살아가고 있습니다. 부모가 되고 나니, 비로소 부모의 마음을 조금은 알 것 같습니다.

    홀로 계신 엄마가 더 자주 생각납니다. 엄마는 무척 꽃을 좋아하셨습니다. 그리고, 엄마 자신이 바로 우리 삶에 피워 주신 가장 아름다운 꽃이셨습니다.

They say that parents are gardeners, tending the trees that God has entrusted to them— the children. In the garden nurtured by my mother's and father's love, we have each blossomed into fragrant flowers, blooming in our own corners of the world.

Now, my own son and daughter have quietly grown into young adults in their twenties. As I look at them—still so young in my eyes— my thoughts turn once more to Mother, who bore the weight of life and built a home at an even younger age. And my heart swells with a deeper, fuller respect. I wonder, what kind of seeds am I planting in my children's hearts?

I am a gardener, too—one appointed by our Heavenly Father. With the nourishment of wisdom, the warmth of love, and the careful watering of devotion, I tend to these lives, so they may one day. Now, the children once held in my arms are becoming parents themselves, learning to stand strong against the winds of this world. And as I walk the path of parenting, I begin to understand— just a little more—the heart of my own parents.

As the month of family draws to a close, I find myself thinking more often of my mother, who now lives alone. She truly loved flowers. And in truth, she was the most beautiful flower ever to bloom in the garden of our lives.

흔들리는 바나나 잎
-온도이 빌리지 예수.11

김동욱

먹먹한 땅에 유령처럼 머리를 풀어헤친 삭쾡이 바람이 비를 데몰고 달려왔다 바나나 잎이 부수수 흔들리기 시작했다 코코넛 나무 아래 나른한 오후를 졸던 피부병 걸린 몇 몇 개들은 낯선 손님인 듯 하늘 향해 컹컹컹 꼬리를 좌우로 흔들며 얕은 나무 아래 몸을 숨겼다

바나나 잎에 세찬 빗방울 떨어질 때마다 우워웡 먹구름을 뚫고 수천 볼트에 감전된 듯 소리 점점 커지며 수 갈래 아버지 심장같은 울림 온도이 빌리지를 찾은 청년 예수의 긴 머리와 낡은 도포자락을 적시고 있었다

Shaking Banana Leaves
-Ondo Yi Village Jesus, 11

Kim Dongouk

The ghostly wind, wild and unrestrained, Ran with the rain, loosening its tangled hair, The banana leaves began to shake, crumpling under the weight. Underneath the coconut trees, Lazy afternoons slept on the backs of the afflicted, Those with sores like forgotten whispers, They trembled as strange guests approached, Their tails wagging, eyes toward the sky, Hiding their fragile bodies beneath shallow branches.

Every time the rain pounded the banana leaves, A deep, thunderous cry pierced through the dark clouds, Like a thousand volts of lightning, The sound grew louder, splitting like the heart of a father. In the midst of it all, The young Jesus of Ondo Yi Village, His long hair and worn cloak soaked through, Bore the storm with silent grace

바람 커지고 흔들림 거세지며 잎새 찢긴다 바나나 이파리 만갈래 찢기며 흔들려 운다 빵을 주세요 칼을 주세요 이땅에 왕국을! 외면치 마세요 창빛 바램을 빵으로 찬 왕국, 번개도 수백 번 돌아야 이르를 수 있어요 아버지 꿈이 바나나 상처 감쌀 수 있나요

청년 예수의 아미에 파르르 경련이 일었다 잘려나간 바나나 목에서 몇 방울 파리한 눈물 예수의 이마를 지나 무릎 발등에 앉았다 찌지직 쾅쾅 하늘을 가르고 천둥 번개 온도가 빌리지 울고 있는 땅을 지나갔다 흔들리는 바나나 잎 보며 가슴을 쓸어내렸다 청년 예수, 한없이 한없이 비가 내렸다 그날 따라

The wind swells, the trembling grows fierce, Leaves tear apart, banana leaves ripped to pieces, Crying out in pain, "Give us bread, give us the sword! A kingdom on this earth!" Do not turn away, The light of hope shines in bread, A kingdom crowned by lightning— But even the bolts must strike a hundred times to find their mark. Can the Father's dream heal the wounds of a banana leaf?

In the young Jesus' army, a tremor runs through, A tear falls from the severed banana neck, A pale drop of sorrow that passes through Jesus' brow, Settling on His knees, His feet.
Crackling, clashing—thunder splits the sky, Lightning tearing through, And the land of Ondo Yi Village, weeping beneath,
As the wind howls, and the banana leaves tremble. The young Jesus, endlessly, endlessly—The rain fell that day, a downpour without end.

신앙 시의 목소리

김동욱

일반시를 쓰는 이들을 향해서는 무어라 말 할 수 없다. 문학이
그들의 성(Castle)일 수 있고, 기쁨일 수 있고, 자존감일 수 있고,
살아있음의 근거일 수 있고, 시인임을 입증하는 것이기에,
그들은 얼마든지 낭만을 즐기고, 분위기를 찾고, 감정을 표출
할 수 있다.

그러나 신앙시를 쓰는 이들은 뭔가 좀 다른 목소리의 시를 써야
하지 않을까 생각해 본다. 신앙시를 쓰는 작가들은 신앙적인
것만 골라 쓰라는 말이 아니다. 문제는 너무 쉽게 신앙적 주제
들을 표현해 낸다는 말이다.

 자신이 만난 하나님, 자신이 깨달은 진리, 자신의 체험을 머리로
만 이해하고 머리로만 쓴다면, 어떨까 고민해 본다. 물론 보이지
않는 신앙적 진리이기에 보이는 글로 표현하는 것에 대해 무엇이
옳고 무엇이 그르다고 아무도 자로 재듯 정답을 줄 수는 없다.

The Voice of Faith Poetry
by Kim Dong-wook

To those who write secular poetry, I offer no criticism. For them, literature may be their castle, their joy, their dignity, the very proof that they are alive― and that they are poets. They are free to delight in romance, to seek atmosphere, to pour out their emotions.

But I wonder should not those who write faith-based poetry speak with a different voice? I do not mean that Christian poets must only write about religious themes. The concern is this: How easily we express spiritual subjects.

When we write of the God we have encountered, the truths we have discovered, the experiences we hold sacred― what if we only understand them in our minds, and write from the mind alone? Of course, faith is unseen. And so we wrestle with expressing the invisible through visible words. Who, then, can truly measure what is right or wrong as if with a ruler?

그러나, 글은 작가의 삶의 분신이라고 말할 때, 근래에 신앙시라
는 이름하에 너무 쉽게 글들을 표현해 내는 것을 보면서 좀 뭔가
아리한 마음이 든다. 열 달 동안 몸에 넣고 수많은 고통과 아픔과
출산의 수고를 통해 새 생명을 잉태하는 어머니의 고통에 비한다
면 우린 너무 쉽게 시 한편을 통해 하늘의 것들을 전하려 하는 것
아닌가 부끄럽다.

하늘의 것을 전하는 이들, 하늘의 비밀과 신비를 이 땅에 전하는
자들은, 더 고민하고 더 아파하고 더 묵상해야 하지 않을까?
사랑 때문에 자신의 아들을 내 놓은 하나님의 내 놓으심에 비하면
우린 무엇을 투자하며 글을 쓰고 있는가? 고민해 볼 일이다.

내 삶속에 투영된 진리, 내 삶을 통해서 나온 그분의 사랑, 내 영혼을
통해 스며 나온 그분의 자비, 설교 한 편 작성하기 위해서는 일주일
내내 묵상하며 고민하며 기도하며 몸부림 치며 완성하는 목회자들에
비해, 오히려 우리 작가들은 피상적으로, 그분의 사랑을 표현하지
않을까 고민해 본다.

Yet when we say that writing is the imprint of a writer's life, I cannot help but feel a certain ache as I see how easily words are poured out today under the name of "faith poetry." Compared to a mother who carries life in her womb for ten months— enduring pain, sorrow, and the labor of birth— is it not shameful how lightly we try to convey heavenly truths in a single poem?

Those who speak of heavenly things, those who carry the mysteries and secrets of God into this world— shouldn't they wrestle more deeply, grieve more honestly, and meditate more earnestly? When we consider the cost of God's love— that He gave His only Son— what, then, are we offering as we write? It is something worth pondering.

The truth that is reflected through my life, the love of God that flows out through my living, His mercy that seeps through my soul— how can these be expressed lightly? Pastors spend an entire week wrestling in prayer, reflecting deeply, and laboring to prepare a single sermon. And yet we, as writers, might be speaking of divine love in ways that are too shallow, too distant.

크리스천 작가가 되는 첫걸음

김동욱

싱싱한 알을 사다가 삶아 먹으면 잠시 배부르고 만족을 얻을 수 있습니다 그러나 새 생명에 대한 참 만족과 환희를 노래 할 순 없습니다.

20일간 엄마 닭의 품에서 수십 번 돌고 또 돌며 깨어질 준비를 하다가, 어느 순간 알 속에서 수백 번의 몸부림 끝에 드디어 두터운 껍질이 조금씩 깨어지면서 새 생명을 알리는 거대한 일이 시작됩니다.

영어 hatching은 알속에 있던 작은 생명체가 조금씩 자기 몸을 움직이면서 밖으로 나가 새 생명의 완전체로 되기 위한 길고 긴 과정을 말합니다. Hatching 하는 과정이 안쓰럽다고 누군가 밖에서 껍질을 까주거나 없애준다면 빨리 나온 병아리는 얼마 있지 못해 비실비실 쓰러져 죽고 맙니다.

The First Step to Becoming a Christian Writer
by Kim Dong-wook

Buying a fresh egg and boiling it may fill you for a moment—a brief satisfaction, a fleeting sense of fullness. But it can not sing of the true joy and wonder of new life.

For twenty days, a mother hen holds the egg close beneath her wings. Inside, the tiny life turns again and again, preparing to be broken. And then, after countless inner struggles, the thick shell begins to crack— just a little at first —and the great work of proclaiming new life begins.

The English word hatching describes the long and gradual process through which the life within an egg stirs, presses outward, and finally emerges as a full, living being. If someone, feeling pity, were to crack the shell from the outside—if they removed the struggle—the chick, though born quickly, would soon stumble, grow weak, and die.

자신을 둘러 싼 두터운 껍질에서 나오기 위해 수십 번 수백 번 온몸으로 싸우는 긴긴 싸움의 시간을 통해서 새 생명이 이 땅에 나오게 되고 살아서 움직이는 귀여운 병아리를 보며 어린아이들은 소망을 품게 되는 것입니다.

자신을 둘러싸고 있는 수십 수백의 두터운 껍질, 절대 남에게 내놓고 싶지 않은 부끄럽고 숨기고 싶고, 좌절이었던 흑역사 같은 껍질을 한 겹씩 벗겨내는 작업이 진솔한 작가로 서는 과정이라고 봅니다.

타인의 깊은 가슴을 울리고 '그래 그게 바로 나야!! 나도 그랬어 이젠 할 것 같아' 가슴을 치며 웅크렸던 두 다리를 일어서게 만드는 것은 바로 깊은 고난의 골짜기를 견뎌 내고 그 고난까지도 끌어안고 일어서는 부활을 전해 주기 때문입니다.

그렇기에 진정한 크리스천 작가가 되는 첫걸음은 두터운 자신의 껍질을 벗겨내는 것입니다.

Through the long, fierce struggle—hundreds of twists, countless pushes from within— the new life breaks free from the thick shell that surrounds it. And when the living, breathing chick finally appears, children gaze upon it with joy, their hearts filled with hope.

The many thick shells surrounding us— those layers we desperately wish to hide, the shameful, painful histories, the dark past we dare not reveal— peeling these away, layer by honest layer, is the very path to becoming a sincere writer.

What truly moves the hearts of others, what makes someone cry out, "Yes—that's me! I've been there too. And now... maybe I can rise again," what lifts weary legs from their crouch, is not eloquence— but the testimony of one who has endured the deepest valleys of suffering and has embraced even that suffering to rise again in resurrection.

That is why the true first step to becoming a Christian writer is the courage to shed your own thick shell.

소나기

김제순

길을 건너던 어느 순간,
하늘은 눈물처럼 문을 열고 비를 내린다.
어른도 아이도 지나던 그 길,
카라바우 뛰놀던 들길엔
달리는 빗줄기가 자리를 대신한다.

하늘을 걷던 구름 따라
바닷바람은 불어와 물길을 피워낸다.
함께 달리던 친구의 이름을 불러 세워보지만,
젖은 옷과 가벼운 발은 집을 향해
더 바삐 걸음을 재촉한다.

김제순 시인은 백석총회 파송 필리핀 선교사로 현지 교회 설립 및 교육 사역을 하고 있으며, 글로벌선교문학회 회원으로 활동 중입니다.

Sudden Shower
by Kim Je-Soon

While crossing the road one quiet day,
The sky unlatched and wept its way.
Where elders, children used to pass,
And carabaos played through fields of grass,
Now racing rain takes up the space,
Its silver feet a fleeting trace.

Clouds once wandered soft and wide,
As sea-winds stirred the stream's new tide.
I called out loud to my running friend,
But soaked and shivering steps ascend—
Their hurried path now homeward bent,
By rain and chill and shoulders spent.

울먹이던 하늘은
빛으로 답하며 길을 밝히고,
건너야 할 강을 그리워하게 한다.
고국에는 생명이 숨 쉬고,
친구의 소식은 땅 아닌 하늘로만 흐른다.
기다림에 지친 하루,
소나기는 불쑥 문을 열고 찾아든다.

세찬 바람과 함께
요란한 빗방울 속에 친구가 들어온다.
생각은 시간을 넘어 내일의 꿈을 그리며
고개를 젓듯 춤추는 마음,
멈춰 선 걸음은 물길을 바라본다.

The sky, still trembling, answers in light,
Illuminates the path, makes longing bright—
For rivers we've yet to cross again,
For homelands breathing life through rain.
No news from friends upon the ground,
Only heaven echoes their silent sound.
A weary day worn thin with ache,
The sudden shower bursts and breaks.

Through roaring drops and restless air,
A friend arrives, like answered prayer.
Thoughts drift beyond the hands of time,
Sketching dreams in rhythm and rhyme.
The heart, it sways, a gentle no—
And stillness turns to watch the flow.

십자가
김제순

그대는 황혼의 뜰에 가 보았는가
젊음이 빛바랜 붉은 노을로
나무는 죽어라 생명을 접고
한 젊은이를 피투성이가 되게 만든 하루를

하늘에는 먹구름도 싫어서
흑암으로 덮어 버리고
지성소를 지키려던 화려한 완장은
부끄러운 요구에 맨살로 피하고
백부장은 죽어 빛바랜 나무의 노을을 경외하네

노을이
흑암으로 땅에 묻히던 날
태양은 모두를 감추어 버리고
또 하나의 새벽 바위는 스스로의 꿈을 접고
하나의 생명을 토하여 긴 잠을 깨웠네

The Cross
by Kim Jesoon

Have you stood in the courtyard of twilight,
where youth fades into a blood-red sunset?
The tree surrendered life in silence,
and one young man was torn into blood and sorrow that day.

Even the sky, weary of storm clouds,
wrapped itself in utter darkness.
The ornate badge guarding the Holy Place
shrank from shame, stripped bare before the plea.
The centurion, struck by awe,
beheld the faded crimson on that dying tree.

On the day
when the sunset was buried beneath the darkness,
the sun veiled all in silence.
Another dawn, hidden in stone, let go of its dream—
and from it, one life was born again
to awaken us from our long slumber.

동인작가글

몽상으로
김제순

홀로 사는 인생이라
벽이 있어 벽을 넘지 못해
한 밤에 흐느낌의 소리 들려 오지요

누구에게도 보여 줄 수 없어
시야의 강물은 소리없이 흐르고
눈썹에 끼인 안개는 물보라였지요

사랑에 가는 마음
오늘은 열어 보았더니
과거에 오르던 기쁨은 한숨일 뿐

베갯잎 층층히 품어 두었던
님의 행복 베냇저고리 향수엔
몽상으로 바람같은 세월에 버렸네요

Into Reverie
by Kim jesoon

A life lived alone—
walls stand firm, too high to climb,
and in the night, I hear soft sobs echo.

I can not show this to anyone,
so the river of sight flows in silence,
and the mist caught in my lashes
becomes a spray of sorrow.

A heart once drawn to love—
today I opened it, but the joy that
once climbed from the past is now only a sigh.

Layer by layer, my pillow held the scent of your happiness,
wrapped in the memory of a baby's first gown.
But in a breeze-like time,
I cast it away into dreams—into reverie.

어느 봄날의 장터

김진순

따사로운 봄 햇살 윙크로 눈부시다. 들뜬 봄바람 맞아 잔기침하며 깡총깡총 시장에 들어선다. 봄 햇살은 어김없이 긴긴 겨울밤 밤의 초조한 기다림을 기억한다.

흰 고무신 코 고무신 긴 장화들도 보약 한 첩 먹은 듯 밖으로 쏟아져 나온다. 햇빛 따라 자리 잡은 옆집 영희 엄마 좌판대 앞에 엄마가 멈추어 선다. 냉이 쑥... 이름 모를 봄나물들 손 흔들어 녹색 향기를 전해온다.

두터운 겨울 옷 깊은 주머니에서 손을 뺀 영희 엄마의 미소는 봄 햇살 같다. 구수한 된장국 냄새와 함께 이웃의 정을 담은 냉이 봉지를 건네온다. 냉이 따라 시냇물을 건너온 봄바람 바위들을 넘어 푸릇푸릇 들판을 날아간다.

지지배배 종달새와 이름 모를 새들이 상큼한 목소리로 새봄을 노래한다. 장터에서 돌아오는 길, 철축 꽃망울은 수줍어 얼굴을 숨기는데, 산수화는 노오란 웃음을 건네며 봄 장터 이야기 전해 달란다.

김진순 사모는 CCC 은퇴 후 현재 경기 광주 베델교회 사모, 네팔 성토 신학교 교수, 글로벌선교문학회 회원으로 활동 중이다.

A Spring Day at the Market
by Jinsoon Kim

The warm spring sun winks, dazzling my eyes. Tickled by the giddy spring breeze, I hop and skip into the market. The sunlight, ever faithful, remembers the restless longing of long winter nights.

White rubber shoes, old worn boots, and tall rain boots spill out onto the street, as if revived by a healing tonic. By the stall where Young-hee's mother sits, my own mother pauses. She reaches for shepherd's purse, mugwort, and nameless greens that wave their hands, sending whispers of green-scented joy.

Young-hee's mother, her hands freed from deep winter coat pockets, smiles a smile warm as the morning sun. With the earthy scent of soybean soup lingering in the air, she hands us a bag of spring herbs, wrapped in neighborly love. The breeze that crossed the stream with the shepherd's purse leaps over rocks and dances through green fields.

Chirping skylarks and birds without names sing sweet songs of a newborn spring. On the way home from the market, azalea buds hide their blushing faces, while golden cornelian cherry flowers smile and whisper: "Won't you share the story of the spring market with me?"

내가 선택한 평안

김진순 사모

최근 나는 특별한 분을 만났다.
그는 나를 송두리째 뒤흔든 분이다.
천천히 자족하며 안전을 추구하려는 내게
다른 세계를 보여 주었다.

그는 선교사로 사역한 후, 미국에서 더 공부했다.
미국에서 목회를 했고, 지금은 협동 목사로 섬기신다.
본업은 헬라어 히브리어 교수이시다.

나도 온라인에서 그분에게 원어를 배운다.
한 단어 한 단어를 분해하며 잘 가르치신다.
그분은 예수님처럼 살고, 가난하게 사는 것을
좌우명으로 여기신다. 자가용이 없다.
세 자녀는 대학을 졸업했고 결혼했으며,
사역자도 있다.

The Peace I Chose
by Kim Jin-sun

Recently, I met a remarkable person—
someone who shook me to the core.
As I sought a slow, contented, and secure life,
he unveiled a different world before me.

He served as a missionary,
then pursued further studies in the U.S.
He pastored a church there
and now serves as an associate pastor.
His main profession is teaching Greek and Hebrew.

I, too, learn biblical languages from him online,
where he skillfully breaks down each word with precision.
He lives like Jesus,
embracing poverty as his life's creed.
He owns no car.
His three children have all graduated,
married, and some are serving in ministry.

교수님과 사모님을 점심 식사에 초대했다.
두 분은 각자 자전거를 타고 식당에 오셨다.
추운 날이었다. 미끄러워 보이는 곳도 드문드문 있었다.
사모님은 구독자 십 만 명이 넘는 유튜브 요리 강사이다.
교수님은 맛있는 음식을 매일 먹는다고 자랑하신다.
살림은 전적으로 사모님이 하시는 것 같다.
가난을 지향하는 남편을 좋아하는 아내가 존경스러웠다.
나의 세계를 흔들었고 내 삶을 돌아보았다.

나는 그리스도인으로 예수님처럼 사는가?
예수님처럼 살기를 소원하는가?
나도 그분처럼 청결을 좇아 살아가고 있는가?
50여 년 전 처음 회심했을 때, 순종을 결심하며
첫사랑으로 눈을 뜨자마자 말씀을 읽었다.
길이요 진리요 생명이신 말씀을 붙잡고 기도했다.
그리고 기도 응답을 많이 받았다. 앞길을 인도받았다.
집안 유전인 당뇨병도 20대에 기도로 치유 받았다.
불신 가정에서 성장한 나는, 믿음만 보고 결혼했다.

I invited the professor and his wife for lunch.
They each arrived at the restaurant on their bicycles.
It was a cold day, with patches of slippery ground here
and there. His wife is a YouTube cooking instructor
with over a hundred thousand subscribers. The professor
proudly claims he enjoys delicious meals every day.
It seems she takes full charge of the household.
I deeply respected this woman who loves a husband
devoted to poverty. They shook my world, and I reflected
on my own life.

Do I, as a Christian, truly live like Jesus?
Do I earnestly desire to live as He did?
Do I also pursue purity as he does?
When I first encountered Christ fifty years ago,
I resolved to obey Him. Awakening to my first love,
I began each day with Scripture. I clung to the Word—
the Way, the Truth, and the Life— and prayed fervently.
Many prayers were answered, and my path was guided.
Even the hereditary diabetes in my family
was healed through prayer in my twenties.
Raised in a non-believing home, married solely by faith.

그런데 처음 사랑을 언제 버렸나? 세상과 짝하던 날들이 눈앞을 스친다. 주님 앞이나 세상에 특출하다고 내놓을 것이 없다. 자녀가 방황하고 있다. 순간 낙망하며 한순간 마음이 무너져내렸다. 낙심 속에서, 독감에 걸려 앓아누웠다.

누워 말씀을 들을 때였다. 일상생활이 소중하다는 생각이 번뜩 들었다. 밥하고 청소하는 이런 일상도 소중하다. 주님의 뜻대로 순종하려고 노력하는 것 뛰어나지 않더라도, 아직 풀리지 않은 여러 문제가 있더라도 인내하고 기도하는 삶이 소중함을 깨달았다

창문을 여니 하얀 눈이 온 땅을 감싸고 있다
존경하는 그분의 영혼같은 눈이 먼지 가득한
세상을 덮고 있다 전거를 타고 먼저 떠나시는
사모님의 안전을 위해 조심스레 두 손을 모은다

But when did I forsake my first love? Memories flash
before me—days when I walked hand in hand with the
world. I have nothing remarkable to offer before the
Lord or the world. My children are wandering.
In that moment, despair crept in, and my heart crumbled.
Weighed down by discouragement, I fell ill with the flu.

As I lay there listening to the Word, a sudden realization
struck me—. the beauty of ordinary life.Even cooking,
cleaning, and daily routines are precious.
Though I may not excel, though unanswered struggles
remain, a life of patience and prayer,
striving to obey His will, is invaluable.

I open the window— white snow blankets the earth.
Like the pure soul of the one I admire, it covers this
dust-laden world. As she rides ahead on her bicycle,
I clasp my hands gently in prayer for her safe journey.

노년의 행복

김진순

신선한 바람으로 머리칼을 날리며 목현천을 따라 걷는다. 외출만으로 운동이 충분하다는 생각을 바꾸었다.
시간 정해 산책길을 걸으면서 뿌듯함을 느낀다.
정신이 맑아진다. 주위를 둘러보는 재미도 솔솔하다.
어느덧 일흔이 넘었다. 뒤편에서 기러기 날아 내 곁을 지나간다. 이전에는 날아가는 기러기가 이렇게 쓸쓸한지 몰랐다. 이별이 머리를 스친다. 옆에서 보아도 보아도 또 보고 싶고, 보고픈 얼굴들이다.

소풍 갈 때 꼭 필요하고 맛있는 것만 챙기듯, 저문 시간 나와 동행할 옷가지나 생필품 등을 챙긴다. 찾아 쓰기도 번거롭다. 꼭 필요한 좋은 물건만 추린다. 내가 이렇게 부자인 줄 몰랐다. 이제야 넉넉함을 누린다.

The Happiness of Old Age

by Kim Jin-sun

A fresh breeze tousles my hair as I walk along Mokhyeon Stream. I have changed my mind—going out is not enough exercise. Setting aside time for a daily walk brings me quiet satisfaction. My mind feels clearer, and I enjoy observing the world around me. I have now passed seventy. From behind, a flock of geese takes flight, soaring past me. I never realized before how lonely their journey seemed. Thoughts of farewell cross my mind. No matter how often I see them, the faces I cherish remain ones I long to see again.

Just as we pack only the essentials for a picnic,
I gather what I need for the journey ahead a few garments, simple necessities. Even searching for things has become a task, so I keep only what is truly valuable. I never knew I possessed so much. Only now do I truly embrace abundance.

남편에게 불평한 일들이 생각난다. 넥타이 색으로 이른
아침부터 불평했다. 많은 넥타이에서 더 멋진 것이 탐났다.
보석보다 귀한 젊음의 많은 시간을 그렇게 어두움으로
낭비했다. 불평할 힘까지 넘치던 아주 좋은 세월이었다.
그런 것이 뭐 대수라고!

아침마다 불평으로 인사받으며 집 떠나는 마음은 어땠을까?
그것이 나의 사랑 표현이었을까? 사랑받는다고 느꼈을까?
패션 감각이 뛰어난 딸은 어떻게 했지? 내가 옷을 곱게
입고 나설 때면, 말없이 웃으며 나를 바라보던 딸, 얼른
한두 개의 옷을 내와서 코디해주던 딸의 반짝임이 대조된다.
나는 사랑하는 대신 사랑을 받았다.

I recall the complaints I once voiced to my husband.
One morning, I grumbled over the color of his tie.
With so many ties to choose from, I longed for something finer. Precious years of youth—more valuable than jewels— were squandered in the shadows of such trivial discontent.
Back then, I had energy even for complaints. What a waste of those good and abundant days! How must he have felt, leaving home each morning to the sound of my dissatisfaction?

Was that how I expressed love?
Did he ever feel truly cherished?
And what about my daughter, with her keen sense of style?
Whenever I dressed up,
she would simply smile, watching me in silence.
Then, without a word, she would bring a piece or two
to complete my outfit, her presence sparkling with warmth.
What a contrast—she gave love effortlessly,
while I only knew how to receive it.

아름다운 아들 딸을 주신 복이 내 능력인 양, 어깨를 들썩거렸다.
딸이나 아들이 좀 더 완전해지기를 소망하며 잔소리했다.
나와 다르다고 불평했다. 피서린 상채기가 빤히 보인다.
용서 구하기에 정신없이 바쁜 나날이다.

이제야 다름에서 뛰어남이 보이니 감사하다. 아직도 방황하는
딸까지 진실로 자랑스럽다. 거울에서 보는 또 다른 나.
자녀손들이 눈에 보이기 시작한다. 뛰어나서가 아니다. 바라볼
때마다 다양한 신비로움에 즐겁다. 놀란다. 살아있어 고맙다.
미우나 고우나 정겹고 고맙고 믿음이 간다. 내 마음을 기댄다.

평생 님께 거저 받아 누리는 분에 넘치는 사랑! 노년에
어떻게 흘려보낼까요? 이 생각 저 생각에 눈웃음 날린다.

I once swayed with pride, as if the blessing of my
beautiful children were a reflection of my own merit.
Hoping they would be more perfect, I nagged and criticized,
finding fault in their differences from me.
Now, I see the wounds I inflicted, so stark, so undeniable.
These days, I am busy seeking forgiveness. At last, I have
come to see the brilliance in their uniqueness, and for that,
I am grateful.

Now, I see my grandchildren more clearly— not because
they excel, but because they surprise me, delight me,
with the quiet mysteries of who they are.
They make me grateful to be alive. Whether flawed or
flawless, they are dear, they are precious, and I find
myself leaning into them with trust.

A lifetime of love—freely given, undeserved, abundant.
How shall I let it flow in my later years?
I smile at the thought, as laughter lingers in my eyes.

심연
노희설

다가왔다 물러갔다
하루 해가 지고
수십 번 달이 머물다 가고
해가 바뀌어도
으르렁 처얼썩

헤아릴 수 없는 깊이에는
정적보다 깊은
고요가 흐르고
세상 다 흔들어 봐
그저 피어낸 웃음

네가 나를 알고
내가 너를 품에 안아
억겁으로 기다리는
시간의 고요

노희설 선교사는 1997년 필리핀 파송 이후 28년 동안 교회개척. 신학교 사역. 아시아 선교회 사역 중. 지구촌 선교문학회 회원이며 워십팀 에이레네 단원으로 활동 중이다.

Abyss

by Noh Hee-Seol

Draws near, then fades away,
the sun departs, the moon returns
countless nights, relentless tides,
years may turn, yet still they roar,
a ceaseless, thunderous hush.

In depths beyond all measure,
silence flows, profound and pure.
Let the world tremble, let it break
the abyss responds with quiet laughter,
unmoved, eternal, whole.

You know me, and I embrace you,
held in waiting, bound in time
a hush unbroken, deep with longing,
eternity's unspoken breath.

바람
노희설

스쳐 가지만 느낄 수 없어요
꽃들이 환하게 웃고
풀들이 소근거리니
바람인 줄 알아요

스쳐 가지만 알 수 없어요
향긋한 꽃 내음과
싱그런 풀 내음이
온몸을 휘감으니
바람이 온 줄 알아요

스쳐 가지만 볼 수 없어요
구름이 흘러가고
달이 산 어귀에
보이다 숨었다 하니
바람이 다가오는 줄 알아요

흔들리지만 볼 수 없어요
청보리가 눕고 일어나
도란도란 흔들릴 때
내 마음도 흔들리니
바람이 머문다 간 줄 알아요

The Wind
by Noh Hee-Seol

It brushes past, yet I can not see,
but flowers bloom in radiant cheer,
and grasses whisper soft and low—
so I know the wind is here.

It drifts by, yet I can not tell,
but fragrant blooms and verdant fields
embrace me in their sweet embrace—
so I know the wind draws near.

It passes by, yet I can not gaze,
but drifting clouds and hiding moon
appear, then vanish through the hills—
so I know the wind is near.

It stirs, yet I can not behold,
but barley bends, then stands again,
soft murmurs waltz in golden waves—
and as my heart sways in its song,
I know the wind has lingered long.

내 생애 가장 소중한 선물
노희설

그녀를 자매라는 인연으로 만난 것은 내 생에 가장 소중한 선물 중의 하나다. 오래전부터 꿈꿔왔던 것은 우리 둘만의 여행이었다. 수십 년의 세월 동안 사는 나라가 다르다는 이유로 잠시 만나는 것도 여의치 않았고, 소식을 주고받는 것도 시간을 쪼개서 사용하는 그녀에게 부담이 될 것 같아 망설이다 어쩌다 연락을 하곤 했다.

아니다, 아무리 긴 시간 이야기를 나누어도 퍼내도 퍼내도 끝없이 솟아나는 샘물처럼 이야기는 한계가 없어서 늘 아쉬움만 남았다. 그 갈증을 해소하고 싶어 찾은 방법이 일상을 떠나 낯선 곳에서 그녀와 보내는 몇 날 며칠에 대한 기대감이었다. 수년 동안의 간절함은 현실이 되었고 그렇게 함께 한 시간은 원했던 것처럼, 바랬던 것보다 충분하게 마음과 감성을 채웠다. 우리는 그곳에서 과거로 거슬러 어린 시절 한적하고 고즈넉한 작은 시골 마을로 추억여행을 떠나곤 했다.

과거를 더듬으며 떠올린 기억들을 내가 얼마나 세밀하고 섬세하게 기억하고 있는지 놀라웠다. 어린 시절의 환경은 평생 반추하게 하고 이런저런 상황에서 크고 작게 또는 부정적이든 긍정적이든 영향을 미치는 것을 부인할 수 없을 것이다. 그 시절 떠오른 기억의 대부분은 그녀와 관련된 장면들이다. 두 살 터울의 자매로 함께 보낸 시간이 절대적으로 많았고 같은 사연을 공유하고 있었기 때문이리라.

The Most Precious Gift in My Life
By Noh Hee-seol

Meeting her and calling her sister—that, I believe, is one of the most precious gifts my life has given me. For many years, I dreamed of a journey just for the two of us. But living in different countries meant even brief meetings were rare. I often hesitated to reach out, worried that even exchanging letters might become a burden for her, who always carved out time so carefully.

Yet whenever we did speak—no matter how long—it never felt like enough. Our conversations were like a wellspring: no matter how much we poured out, more memories, more laughter, more stories would rise. And so, my longing only deepened. To quench that thirst, I dreamed of spending a few quiet days with her, away from the routines of daily life, in a place unfamiliar, where it could be just the two of us. That longing, carried over the years, finally blossomed into reality. And our time together—more than I had wished, exactly as I had hoped—filled my heart and spirit so fully. In that space, we often wandered back through time—revisiting the peaceful little village of our childhood.

It amazed me how clearly I could recall even the tiniest of details. Childhood shapes us deeply—its echoes lasting throughout our lives, casting shadows or light in both subtle and profound ways. And in those memories, almost every image that surfaced had her in it. We were just two years apart, always together, sharing nearly every moment, every story. It's no wonder so many of those memories were hers as much as they were mine.

내가 기억하는 그녀는 어려서부터 누가 가르쳐주지 않아도 모든 것을 참 잘했다. 공부도 잘해서 늘 우등상을 받고 달리기도 잘하고 글짓기도 잘하고 그림도 잘 그려서 교내외 상도 받았으며 촌에서 유일하게 소유할 수 있었던 악기 피리도 곧잘 불었고 붓글씨도 잘 썼으며 그녀의 작품이 늘 교실 뒷편에 걸려있었다. 힘겨운 농사일을 갈무리하고 늦은 저녁 지친 몸으로 집에 돌아온 부모님께 큰 딸이 내민 성적표와 상장은 피곤한 부모님의 행복과 큰 웃음이 되었다.

어느 날 이순신 장군에 대한 글짓기가 숙제로 주어졌고 나도 작문을 잘 써서 상장을 받아 부모님께 웃음꽃 한 아름 안겨드리고 싶은 욕심에 머리를 싸매고 문장을 찾아 헤매던 중 언니 국사 교과서에 나온 이순신 장군에 대한 글을 발견하고 그 글을 베끼고 나의 생각을 덧붙여 제출했고 교내 대표 작문으로 선정되었다. 어느 날 우연히 내 원고지를 그녀가 보게 되었고 내 글짓기가 교과서 글을 따왔다는 것을 단번에 알아보고 얼마나 호되게 야단을 치던지 민망하고 창피하고 뭔지 모를 억울함에 눈물을 훔쳤다.

그 이후로는 한 번도 그런 어리석은 일을 하지 않았다. 초등학교 4학년 때부터는 교내에 문학반 클럽이 생겨서 일상을 주제로 글을 쓰고 문학반 선생님께 칭찬도 받고 내 글이 친구들에게 낭독되어지기도 했다. 그 일이 오히려 글에 대한 열망을 갖게 하였고 소소한 성취를 통해 성장을 가져올 수 있는 고마운 사건이었다.

The sister I remember was always effortlessly good at everything, even from a young age. No one had to teach her—she just knew. While our mother toiled in the fields, it was she who prepared our evening meals. She was a top student, always winning academic awards. She ran fast, wrote beautifully, drew with skill, and even played the only musical instrument anyone in the village owned—a recorder—with ease. Her calligraphy was so elegant that her works often hung proudly at the back of the classroom. When our parents came home late from a long day's labor in the fields, weary and sunworn, it was her report cards and certificates that lit up their faces with laughter and joy.

One day, we were assigned an essay on Admiral Yi Sun-sin. I longed to win an award too—to make my parents beam with pride, just as she did. So I wrestled with words, searching for inspiration, and in the end, I copied a passage from her history textbook, added some of my own thoughts, and submitted it. To my surprise, it was selected as the school's representative essay. But then, she happened to read my manuscript. In an instant, she recognized the borrowed words—and scolded me fiercely. I remember how embarrassed and ashamed I felt… and somehow, quietly hurt too.

After that, I never made such a foolish choice again. In fourth grade, a literature club was formed at school, and we were encouraged to write about our everyday lives. I joined and began sharing my little stories. The teacher praised my writing, and sometimes my work was even read aloud to the class. Looking back, that painful moment became a turning point—a blessing in disguise. It awakened in me a love for writing and gave me small but meaningful milestones of growth.

그녀의 탁월함 덕분에 우리 자매는 농촌에서 대도시로 유학길에 올라 중.고등학교, 대학교를 지내며 단둘이 소녀 시절과 사춘기, 성인으로 성장하기까지 긴 여정을 함께 보냈다. 서로 다른 곳에서 직업을 갖고 그 직업도 같은 일을 하고, 남자를 만나고 결혼을 하고 아이를 낳고 지난한 세월을 살아오는 동안 그녀는 나에게 언니가 되고, 엄마가 되고, 인생 선배가 되고, 친구가 되고 멘토가 되었다.

우리는 문학과 영화, 연극과 전시를 함께 누리며 예민하고 외롭던 시절의 감성을 예술로 달랬다. '별이 빛나는 밤에' 라디오에 설레며 가난한 마음을 위로받았고, 예술은 우리에게 따뜻한 쉼터였다. 지금도 그녀는 시와 책을 나눠주며 나의 관심과 기호를 섬세히 살핀다. 그녀가 건네는 글은 내 삶의 방향이 되고, 깊이와 성숙함을 더해 주는 가장 따뜻한 선물이다.

꽃들이 피고 지고 해가 뜨고 사라지는 것을 바라보며 우리의 지나온 세월도 현재도 다가올 날들도 피고 지고, 뜨고 사라짐이 허무가 아니고 흐르는 강물이라며 연민 할 것이다.

Thanks to her exceptional nature, we, two sisters from a small farming village, found ourselves studying in a big city—walking the long path of adolescence and young adulthood side by side through schooling. Along that journey, we became more than sisters. She was my older sister, and like mother, my role model, my friend, and my lifelong mentor.

We found solace in art during our sensitive and lonely youth —reading literature, watching films and plays, visiting exhibitions, and listening to Midnight Night Music Camp. Through these shared moments, we softened the ache of absence and nurtured our hearts. Even now, she sends me poems and books she knows I'll love, gently curating beauty for my soul. Her thoughtful offerings continue to guide my path, deepening my spirit and adding grace to the weight of years—a gift of quiet, enduring love.

As we watch the flowers bloom and fade, the sun rise and disappear, we learn to see our passing years—the days behind, the moments now, and the time to come—not as futility but as a flowing river. And we hold one another in quiet empathy.

여행에서 처음으로 맞이한 서서히 떠오르던 태양이 아침의 고요를 그토록 눈부시게 깨우고 찬란한 빛으로 존재를 드러낸 것처럼, 우리의 길고 긴 모든 순간들도 아름다움으로 각인될 것이다. 무슨 이야기를 나누고 어떤 장소에서 얼마나 아름다운 창조물에 감탄했는지는 아지랑이 처럼 아른거릴지라도 말이다. 우리가 함께했던 여행은 마침이 아니라 시작이며 다가올 날들에 대한 기다림일 것이다.

연륜은 깊어지고 남아있는 연수는 적어질수록 우리의 영혼을 가꾸고 진리에 대한 갈망을 찾아 끝없이 탐구하고 믿으며 끝내는 그날이 다가와도 또다른 나라를 사모하며 소망함으로 받아들일 것이다.

슬픔의 한자락인 우리의 어머니를 붙들고 내내 설움을 초연한 것처럼 보여지기를 바랄 수 있음은 그녀를 자매라는 인연으로 만나 그 서글픈 세월을 함께 한 나의 언니가 있음이요, 그녀가 내 생에 가장 소중한 선물중의 하나로 언제나 내곁에 남아 사소하고 보잘 것 없는 것일지언정 함께 사유할 수 있기 때문이리라.

On that journey, the first sunrise I witnessed slowly emerged, breaking the morning's stillness with a brilliance that dazzled and awakened everything in sight. Just like that radiant dawn, every moment we shared in those few days will remain etched in beauty—perhaps the words we exchanged or the wonders we admired will blur like a distant shimmer, yet their essence will stay with us. Our journey was not an ending, but a gentle beginning—an invitation to look forward to days yet to come.

As our years deepen and the days ahead grow fewer, our souls long more earnestly for truth, seeking it with open hearts, and when the final day arrives, we will receive it not with fear but with hope, yearning for another home beyond.

And if I appear to hold my sorrow with grace—carrying our mother's fragment of sadness with a calm resolve—it is only because I've been given the gift of her: my sister in this life, who has walked beside me through those aching years. She is one of the most precious blessings of my life, always near, sharing even the smallest of thoughts, quietly and deeply, together.

주여 오늘도
문미숙

주여 오늘도
나의 행위를 바르게 하여
주의 길을 걷게 하소서

이웃을 향한 나의 눈이
봄날의 따사로운 미소이게 하시고
때 묻은 손 내미는 길거리 소년에겐
허기진 배 채우는 포근한
밤 고구마 사랑이게 하소서

주여 오늘도 내 마음이
높고도 맑은 가을 하늘이게 하소서
푸르른 하늘 위에 두둥실 떠가는
하얀 뭉게구름 되어
삶에 지쳐 쓰러진 영혼의 심령에
새 소망의 노래이게 하소서

주여 오늘도 내 영혼이
당신으로 인하여 기뻐 춤추게 하소서
그 영원한 나라 꿈꾸며
새하얀 눈꽃 행복의 나래를
마음껏 펼치게 하소서

문미숙 선교사는 필리핀 31년 자비량 사역중이며 현지 목회, 어성경 전임강사, 지구촌 선교문학회 회원, 워십댄스팀 에이레네 단원 및 오카리나 팀으로 주님을 섬기고 있다

Lord, This Day Again
by Moon Mi-sook

Lord, this day again, I pray,
Guide my steps in truth and way.
Let me walk where You have trod,
Firm in justice, close to God.

May my gaze to others shine,
Soft as springtime's warmest sign.
May my hands to those in need,
Be love that fills where hunger pleads.

Lord, this day again, I yearn,
Make my heart like autumn's sky
Vast and bright, where white clouds turn,
Drifting hope to souls that sigh.
To the weary, bowed and weak,
Let me be the song they seek.
Floating high where dreams take flight,
Singing faith in morning light.

Lord, this day again, I sing,
Let my soul in gladness ring.
Dreaming of Your kingdom bright,
Dancing free in snowflake white.

인생은 품앗이란다!!!

문미숙

"딴다란딴 딴다란딴 딴, 딴다란딴 딴다란딴 딴~~"
"어? 웬일이야?"
"응~언니! 엄마랑 아부지 집에 다녀 왔어."
"어 그래~?"
"근데 언니! 우리 엄마는 어쩜 저러지?"
"왜?"
"있잖아~내가 엄마 목욕시켜드렸거든?"
"응 근데?"
"내가 엄마 목욕시켜드리면서 '엄마! 옛날에는 엄마가 날 이렇게 목욕시켜 줬는데 이제 내가 엄마 목욕시켜드리네~~' 이랬더니 우리 엄마 뭐라고 하시는 줄 알아?"

"뭐라고 하시는데?
'그랑께 인생은 품앗이란다' 엄마가 이렇게 말하는 거 있지. 어떻게 우리 엄마는 그런 생각을 다 하셨을까? 난 우리 엄마 한 번씩 이렇게 말할 때 마다 깜짝 깜짝 놀란다 언니! 진짜 우리 엄마 지혜롭지 않아?"

그랬다. 우리 엄마의 인생은 평생이 돌려받지 못할 품앗이 인생이였다. 가정을 위한 품앗이, 남편을 위한 품앗이, 5남매를 키우기 위한 품앗이.....

Life is a Mutual Giving!

By Moon Mi-sook

"Ddan-da-ran-ddan, ddan-da-ran-ddan-,
"Huh? Whats going on?"
"Oh, sis! I just got back from Mom and Dad's house."
"Oh, really?"
"But sis! How can Mom be like that?"
"What do you mean?"
"You know, I gave Mom a bath today."
"Yeah? And then?"
"As I was washing her, I said, 'Mom! You used to bathe me like this when I was little, and now I'm the one giving you a bath.' And do you know what Mom said?"

"What did she say?"

"She said, 'That's why life is a mutual giving.'
Can you believe that? How did she come up with something like that? Every time she says things like this, I'm
just amazed, sis! Isn't she so wise?"

Yes, she was right. My mother's life had always been one of giving, never expecting anything in return. A life of giving for her family, for her husband, for raising her five children…

엄마!!!
내 가슴속에 새겨진 "엄마"란 단어는 늘 아리하고 시릿한 느낌이다.
처녀 때 그 예뻤던 얼굴도, 찬송가 부르며 고귀하게 다녔던 교회도
시집이란 삶을 살아가며 모두 다 반납하고 단 한번도 꾀를 피우거나
엄살을 부릴 줄도 모른 채 당신 몸이 부서져라 일하고 또 일하며 가정
을 꾸려가고 5남매를 키워냈던 엄마!!!

찬바람 쌩쌩부는 겨울, 새벽을 헤집고 바다를 향해 발걸음을 옮겨
굴을 따오고, 하루 종일 쭈그리고 앉아 굴을 깨 시장에 내다 팔고,
이른 봄 새벽엔 찬 기운 온몸으로 맞으며 밭을 향해 발걸음을 옮겨
새벽 일을 하고 돌아와 아침상을 차리고, 한여름 뙤약볕에 얼굴
그을려가며 밭을 메고 논 일을 하던 엄마!

가을 추수 끝자락 찬바람에도 아랑곳없이 끝도 없는 농사일에
집안일을 도맡아 하며 몸이 부서져 신경통으로 끙끙 앓다가도
아침엔 여전히 자리를 차고 일어나 가족을 위해 아궁이에 불을
지피던 엄마!

The word "Mom"
engraved in my heart always carries a bittersweet ache.
The once-beautiful face of a young maiden,
The noble steps that once walked to church, singing hymns—
All were left behind in the life of marriage.
Never once did you complain, never once did you seek rest.
Instead, you worked and worked, as if your body could break,
Building a home, raising five children—our mother!

In the biting winter winds, before dawn had even broken,
You walked toward the sea to gather oysters,
Spent entire days crouched, cracking them open to sell at the market.
In the early spring mornings, when the chill clung to your bones,
You left for the fields, returning only to prepare breakfast.
In the scorching heat of summer, your face burned beneath the relentless sun As you weeded the fields, toiled in the paddies.

And in the final days of autumn's harvest,
Unfazed by the bitter winds, you labored on.
Even when your body ached with pain,
Even when neuralgia kept you groaning through the night,
At dawn, you still rose,
Lighting the fire in the hearth—
For us, for your family.

나는 그런 엄마를 바라보며 늘 가슴 한 켠이 시리다 못해 아프고 미어
졌다.

그런 슈퍼우먼 엄마가 이제는 세월을 비켜가지 못하고 어느 새
고령의 나이가 되어 인생의 황혼기를 관광차를 빌려 타고 전국을
관광하는 동네 어르신들과도 못 어울릴 만큼 허리가 망가지고 다리
에 힘이 없어 남들 다 가는 관광도 못가고 여전히 텃밭을 가꾸고
집안일을 하며 인생의 저녁노을이 기울어 간다.

카톡!
"언니 우리 지금 올라가요"
"어~벌써? 나 지금 집에 들어와서 엄마 얼굴이나 보려고 전화
하려고 했는데..."
"........"
"언니! 엄마가 우릴 못 알아봐~"
"어~~?"
"큰언니, 큰오빠, 작은 오빠 까지만 기억하고 언니부터 나는 기억
에 없어."
"그 정도야?"
"응~엄마가 치매약을 잘 안챙겨 드셔서 상태가 엄청 악화 되셨네....."
더 이상 할 말이 없었다.

Looking at my mother, my heart would ache—
not just with sorrow, but with an unbearable pain.

That superwoman, my mother, could not escape the grasp of time.
Now, in the twilight of her years, she can no longer join
the village elders who rent buses to tour the country.
Her back is too frail, her legs too weak.
While others travel and enjoy their days, she remains at home,
tending her small garden, keeping busy with housework,
as the sun of her life slowly sets.

Ka-tok! "Sister, we're on our way up now."
"Oh, already? I just got home—I was about to call Mom to see her face for a bit…" "……"
"Sister! Mom… she doesn't recognize us anymore."
"What…?"
"She remembers our eldest sister, eldest brother,
and younger brother…, but from you and me onward,
she has no memory."
"Is it that bad?"
"Yeah… Mom hasn't been taking her dementia medication properly, and her condition has worsened so much…"
There was nothing more to say.

몇 년 전부터 시작된 엄마의 치매...!!!
그렇게 총명하시고 삶의 지혜로 가득 차 있었던 엄마!!!
온 인생을 고생이란 찬바람이 세차게 밀고 간 것일까? 치매라는 폭풍 앞에 스러져버린 엄마의 기억...

"언니, 언제 한국 올 거야?"
"그러게~~가고 싶은데 마음대로 갈 수가 없네. 교회도, 사업장도 맡기고 갈 사람이 없어서..."

"엄마가 조금이라도 움직일 수 있고 정신이 좀 더 맑을 때 언니 오면 엄마, 아부지 모시고 어디 가까운 온천여행이라도 가면 좋겠다 싶어서..."
"그래 알았어~어떻게든 시간 내 볼게..."

이 약속을 올해는 꼭 지키리라 굳게 마음 먹고 있었건만 올초부터 내 계획은 산산히 무너져 버리고 말았다. 거기에 설상가상 엄마의 기억력은 더더욱 악화되어 이제 아예 나와 동생의 이름도 기억 못하신단다. 무엇으로 엄마의 인생을 보상해 줄 수 있을까?

아무도 갚지 않는 엄마 인생의 품앗이!!!
돌려받지 못한 품앗이 삯을 덩그러니 남겨둔 채 아득히 엄마가 멀어져만 간다.

The dementia that began years ago...!!!
My mother—so bright, so wise, her life filled with an abundance of wisdom. Did the harsh winds of hardship sweep her memories away?

Now, before the raging storm of dementia, her once-sharp mind has crumbled.
"Sister, when are you coming to Korea?"
"I wish I could, but it's not that easy.
I have no one to leave the church or the business with…"

"I was hoping that if you came while Mom could still move, while her mind was still somewhat clear, we could take her and Dad on a short hot spring trip."
"I see… I'll try my best to make time."

I had firmly resolved to keep this promise this year.
But from the very start, my plans were shattered. And to make matters worse, Mom's memory has deteriorated even further. Now, she can no longer remember my name, nor my younger sibling's. How can I ever repay my mother's life?

A lifetime of selfless giving, of unreturned sacrifices.
A debt no one has repaid—, left behind, unpaid,
as she drifts further and further away.

살균소독, 오병이어!!!
문미숙

기도원 문을 열고 나서자 싸아한 아침 공기가 사납게 두 뺨을 할퀴고 지나갔다. 두 시간여 마음을 다해 아뢴 내 마음의 소원을 되씹으며 나는 고개를 숙인 채 집을 향해 걷고 있었다.

"얘야 고개를 들어 하늘을 보아라. 왜 땅만 보며 걷고 있니?" "네에?"

나는 순간 고개를 들어 하늘을 우러러 보았다. 내 눈 앞에 펼쳐진 깡마른 나뭇가지가 시야에 들어 왔다.
"주님! 저 나무는 나뭇잎 마져 다 떨어져 버리고 앙상한 가지만 드러내고 있네요. 아무런 소망도 희망도 보이지 않아요 마치 제 마음처럼요"

" 네 눈엔 그렇게 보이니? 얘야, 저 나무는 지금 살균 소독중이란다."

"네에? 살균 소독중요?" "그렇단다. 살균소독 중"

" 아름답고 화려했던 지난 시간을 뒤로하고 차가운 공기와 비바람, 세찬 눈보라로 몸속에 있는 모든 병충들을 살균소독하는 중이란다. 살균소독이 다 되어지면 어느 따스한 봄날에 다시금 메마른 가지를 뚫고 새 생명의 싹을 틔워 아름다운 열매를 맺어 가겠지"

"아 그렇군요 주님! 그럼 지금 내가 처한 환경과 상황들도 살균소독 중인가요?"

Sanitization, The Five Loaves and Two Fish!!!

by Moon Mi-Sook

As I opened the door to the prayer mountain, the brisk morning air fiercely brushed against my cheeks. With my heart full of prayer, I reflected on the desires I had poured out during my two hours of prayer, walking home with my head lowered.

"Child, lift your head and look to the sky. Why are you walking, only looking at the ground?"

"Huh?"

I suddenly raised my eyes and gazed up at the sky. In front of me, the bare, brittle branches of a tree came into view.

"Lord! The tree has shed all its leaves, leaving only the bare, withered branches. There is no hope, no promise to be seen, just like my heart."

"Do you see it that way? Child, that tree is being sanitized right now."

"Huh? Sanitized?" "Yes, it's in the process of sanitization."

"Leaving behind the beautiful and glorious times of the past, the cold air, the rain, and the fierce snowstorm are now sanitizing all the sickness and pests within your body. Once the sanitization
is complete, on a warm spring day, new buds will break through the withered branches, bringing forth beautiful fruit."

"Ah, I see, Lord! So, is the environment and situation I'm in right now also part of this sanitization process?"

"그렇단다. 힘드니? 어렵고 답답하니? 앞이 암담하여 길이 보이지 않니? 지금은 너의 내일을 위한 살균소독 중이니 조금만 더 인내 하거라 내 사랑하는 딸아!"

후끈 올라오는 재래시장의 습한 공기를 들이마시며 장을 보기 시작했다. 나는 부러 외면하며 야채와 생선, 고기 등 일주일 양식을 사 차에 실었다.

" 다 됐어요" " 네에! 가요" "여보 잠깐만요" " 왜?"

나는 급히 차에서 내려 쌀가게로 갔다. 50키로 짜리 쌀 한 가마를 시켜 차 트렁크에 실었다. 차 옆, 좌판 구르마 위에 놓여 있던 노란 바나나 한 송이가 무척이나 탐스러워 보였다.

" 아저씨, 저 바나나 한송이 주세요."

남편은 동그란 얼굴로 날 쳐다보더니, "지난주에 쌀 샀잖아?" 하고 물었다.

" 여보, 사실 주님이 계속 김 선교사님 집에 쌀 한 가마를 사다 달라고 하시는데 내가 계속해서 돈이 부족하다고 떼를 썼어요. 사실 김 선교사님네 쌀 한 가마를 사다 주면 우리 집 돈이 바닥이 나서요. 그래서 모른 척 무시하려고 차를 탔는데 도저히 주님의 음성을 무시하고 그냥 올 수가 없었어요. 그래서 저 쌀 한 가마 하고 바나나는 김 선교사님네 거예요. 가는 길에 내려 드리고 가요."

"아 그래? 난 지난주에 쌀을 샀는데 왜 또 쌀을 사나 했네. 잘했어. 주님이 하라고 하시면 순종해야지. 우리가 좀 더 허리띠 졸라매면 되지."

"Yes, my dear. Is it hard? Do you feel frustrated and weary? Is the path ahead uncertain, and you can't see the way? Know this: you are in a process of sanitization for your tomorrow. Just a little more patience, my beloved daughter."

Breathing in the humid air of the traditional market, I began shopping. I turned my head away and bought vegetables, fish, and meat for the week's provisions, loading them into the car.
"All done?" "Yes, let's go." "Wait, honey!" "What is it?"

I quickly got out of the car and headed to the rice shop. I ordered a 50-kilo bag of rice and had it loaded into the trunk. A bunch of yellow bananas on the cart next to the car caught my eye, looking so tempting.
"Excuse me, could I have that bunch of bananas?"
My husband, with his round face, looked at me and asked,
"We bought rice last week, didn't we?"
"Honey, the Lord has been asking me to buy a bag of rice for Missionary Kim's family, but I kept making excuses about not having enough money. The truth is, if I buy a bag of rice for them, we'll be left with nothing. So, I tried to ignore it and get into the car, but I just couldn't ignore the Lord's voice. So, the rice and the bananas are for Missionary Kim's family. I'll drop them off on the way."

"Oh, really? I was wondering why we were buying rice again when we just bought it last week. You did well. If the Lord asks us to do something, we should obey. We can just tighten our belts a little more."

집으로 돌아오는 길에 김 선교사님 댁에 들러 초인종을 누르니 큰아들이 나오며 "어, 사모님!" 하며 깜짝 놀란다.

나는 두말도 하지 않고 얼른 남편과 함께 쌀 한가마와 바나나 한송이를 떨궈 주고 "시장 갔다 오는 길에 들렀어~너무 이른 아침이지? 나 갈께." 하고 서둘러 집으로 돌아왔다.

오전 10시 50분, 따르릉~~집 전화벨이 울렸다.

"여보세요, 참빛 어학원 입니다. "
"네에 사모님, 안녕하세요. 여긴 ㅇㅇㅇ 선교사님 댁인데요 다음 주 월요일 부터 우리 학생 3명 하루 6시간씩 영어 맨투맨 수업 스케쥴 좀 잡아주세요~~"

오.....주님!!!!

주님은 공짜가 없으셨다. 쌀 한 가마의 순종과 바나나 한송이의 자진 납부를 오병이어의 역사로 바꾸시는 하나님.....
나는 그 멋지신 하나님과 오늘도 기쁨의 동행을 하며 내 인생의 길을 수놓아 가고 있다.

On the way home, I stopped by Missionary Kim's house and rang the doorbell. Their eldest son came out, surprised, saying, "Oh, Pastor's wife!" Without saying another word, my husband and I quickly unloaded the bag of rice and a bunch of bananas, and I said,

"I just stopped by on the way back from the market. It's so early, right? I'll be going now," and hurried back home.

10:50 AM
Ding-dong~~ The house phone rang.
"Hello, this is True Light Language Academy."
"Yes, Pastor's wife, hello. This is Missionary's house. Could you please arrange a schedule for one-on-one English lessons for our three students, 6 hours a day, starting next Monday?"

Oh... Lord!!!!The Lord never lets anything go for free. The obedience of one bag of rice and a bunch of bananas, He transforms into the miracle of the five loaves and two fish...

I am walking in joy with that amazing God today, weaving the path of my life.

목자의 기도

박상금

주님,
오늘 잃어버린 양을 만나게 하소서.
제게 맡기신, 꼭 찾아야 할 그 한 영혼을 만나게 하소서.
주님의 사랑으로 담대히 다가가게 하시고,
그 사랑을 통해 저 또한 사랑하게 하소서.

그들의 아픔과 슬픔, 기쁨까지 함께 나누게 하시고,
주님의 손길이 머무는 곳으로 제 발걸음을 인도하소서.
예수님처럼 눈물을 닦아주며, 위로를 건네는
참된 친구, 진정한 동행이 되게 하소서.

비록 햇볕이 따갑고, 거센 바람이 몰아쳐도
저의 발걸음이 멈추지 않게 하시고,
입술의 기도가 쉬지 않게 하시며,
제 안에 부어진 주님의 사랑을 아낌없이 나누게 하소서.

주여,
눈물의 기도가 메마르지 않게 하시고,
제 영혼이 주님의 사랑에 늘 떨리게 하소서.
주님과 처음 사랑하던 그날을 기억하게 하시어,
한 영혼을 위해서라면 생명조차도 내어줄 수 있는
참된 목자 되게 하소서.

박상금 선교사는 필리핀에서 코피노 사역과 다문화 가정 사역을 하고 있다. 글로벌선교문학회 회원이며 워십댄스 팀 단원, 오카리나 팀 시르오르 리더로 섬기고 있다.

A Shepherd's Prayer
By Park Sang-Geum

Lord,
Let me meet the lost sheep today.
Lead me to the one soul You've entrusted to me,
The one I must find.
Grant me courage to draw near with Your heart of love,
And let that love flow through me.

Let me share in their pain, their sorrow, and their joy.
Guide my steps to the places where Your hand is at work.
Like Jesus, let me be the one who wipes their tears,
A true friend, a faithful companion.

Even when the sun scorches,
Even when fierce storms arise,
Let my steps not falter, Let my lips not fall silent,
And let me pour out the love of Christ within me,
without reserve.

O Lord,
May the prayers born of tears never run dry.
Let my soul tremble with the love of Christ.
May I always remember the day of our first love,
And become a shepherd who, for even one soul,
Would not hesitate to lay down my life.

기억하니 이쁜이들아, 햇살보다 환하게 웃던 날을?

박상금

사랑하는 아들아, 딸아!

너희들의 환한 미소가 내 마음속에 언제나 빛나고 있단다. 너희들의 작은 손을 잡고 뛰놀던 그날들이, 해맑게 웃으며 아빠, 엄마를 부르던 그 순간들이 마치 어제처럼 선명해. 너희들의 웃음소리는 바람이 되고, 너희들의 발걸음은 햇살이 되어 나를 감싸주고 있구나.

세상은 여전히 바쁘게 돌아가지만, 나는 가끔 시간을 멈추고 너희가 뛰놀던 그 길을 거닐곤 한단다. 너희가 좋아하던 그네 앞에서 너희들을 불러보기도 하고, 함께 달리던 놀이터에서 너희들의 웃음을 떠올려 본다.

기억하니 우리 온 가족이 신나게 놀던 그 날을!
놀이동산에서 신나게 미끄럼틀을 타고, 구름다리를 건너며 손을 흔들던 너희들의 모습이 눈앞에 아른거린다. 바람을 가르며 기차놀이를 하던 너희들의 해맑은 얼굴, 아빠와 함께 달리며 깔깔 웃던 그 순간이 아직도 내 가슴에 남아 있단다.

Do you remember, my sweethearts, the day you smiled brighter than the sun?
by Sanggeum Park

My dearest son, my precious daughter,
Your bright, beautiful smiles still shine in the corners of my heart.
The days when I held your tiny hands and ran beside you,
The moments you called out, "Mommy! Daddy!" with sparkling eyes
― they remain so vivid, as if they happened just yesterday. Your laughter dances like the wind,
and your little footsteps have become sunshine that wraps around me.

Though the world moves on in its busy rhythm, I sometimes stop time and quietly walk the paths you once ran. In front of the swing you loved, I call your names, and at the playground where we raced together, I let the echoes of your giggles fill my soul.

Do you remember, my loves,
the joyful day we spent as one happy family? Sliding down the slides at the amusement park, waving your hands as you crossed the cloud bridge ― your sweet little faces glow in my memory.
The laughter we shared as we played train through the wind,
the moments you ran beside your dad, laughing without a care ―
they are treasures that still live in the warmth of my heart.
Here is your touching and heartfelt message translated into warm, poetic English, with the gentle tone of a loving mother:

임진각에서 보트 타고 놀던 모습, 바이킹 타며 신나게 웃고 맛있는 간식 먹던 그림이 지금도 나의 발길을 향하게 하는 곳이다. 선미는 1학년 때 일하고 돌아온 나에게 팔이 닿지 않으니 의자 위에 올라가서 볶음밥을 맛나게 만들어주었고, 선영이는 나의 꿈속에서 교통사고로 우리가 하늘나라에 왔는데 일어날 수 없는 나를 기도하라고 눈으로 말해준 이쁜 아들 덕분에 열심히 기도하며 행복하게 살고 있단다.

밤마다 꿈마다 함께 하는 사랑하는 내 아이들아!
너희는 언제나 그곳에서, 내 가슴속에서 환하게 웃고 있겠지.
우리는 잠시 떨어져 있지만, 다시 만날 그날을 기다리고 있어. 그날이 오면 우리는 더 크게 웃고, 더 힘차게 뛰놀자. 하늘의 그분과 함께 손을 맞잡고 춤을 추자꾸나. 이별은 순간일 뿐, 우리는 다시 만나 더 밝은 미소로 서로를 꼭 안아줄 테니까.

사랑하는 내 이쁜이들아! 다시 만나 실컷 놀자. 그날까지 나의 사랑을 하늘에 실어 보낸다.

The memories of us riding a boat at Imjingak, your joyful laughter echoing as we soared on the Viking ride,—and the sweet snacks we shared afterward — those pictures still guide my feet back to that place, again and again. I remember little Seonmi, when you were just in first grade — how you climbed onto a chair so you could reach the stove and lovingly made fried rice for me after I came home from work. And Seonyeong, my beautiful boy — in my dream, we had gone to heaven after a car accident. I couldn't move, but you looked at me with eyes full of faith, telling me, "Pray, Mommy." Because of you, I did. And because of you, I live each day with joy and strength.

My beloved children, who visit me in every night and every dream, I know you're still there, smiling brightly in the garden of my heart. Though we are apart for a little while,
I am waiting for the day we meet again. On that day, let's laugh louder,run freer, and dance hand in hand with the One above. This goodbye is only for a moment — we will meet again, and when we do, we'll hold each other with even brighter smiles.

My precious little ones,
let's play to our hearts' content when we meet again.
Until that day comes,

I send all my love to you, carried on the wings of heaven.

동인작가 글

네 눈물 위해 내가 죽었노라

박상금

무대를 환하게 비춰오던 조명이 사라지며 박수 소리가 들려왔다. 숨차게 발을 옮겨 다른 의상을 갈아 입으려 무대뒤로 옮겼다. 다섯 명으로 된 워십댄스 에이레네 팀 모두 옷을 갈아입기 위해 분주하다. 유달리 오늘 따라 가슴이 막힌 듯 편하지 않다. 이마에서부터 땀이 흘러 내려와 어깨와 가슴까지 젖게 한다.

'빨리 갈아입고 마음을 준비해야 할텐데 !!'
"박 선교사님 예수님 의상 잘 챙기세요! 파이팅요"
"네 ~~~"
몇 달을 연습했는데도 오늘따라 내 역할인 예수님의 마음이 내 마음에 와 닿지 않는다. "아버지~~"
옷을 입으면서도 마음은 주춤거리고 있었다.

가늘게 음악소리가 흘러 나왔다 내 가슴팍에 내려앉았다
"무슨 소리일까?" 귀를 곤두세우고 듣기 시작했다

"밤마다 아래로 아래로 제 몸 숨기며 그대를 찾아 떠납니다
 제 안에 감춰진 슬픔 물덩이에 넣어 도둑 걸음으로
 두둥실 아기를 꿈꾸며 수가성 우물가로 발길을 옮깁니다"

For Your Tears, I Died
By Park Sang-geum

As the lights that had brightly illuminated the stage disappeared, the sound of applause echoed. Breathing heavily, I hurriedly moved backstage to change into another outfit. The five members of the worship dance team, Eirene, were all busy changing their clothes.

For some reason, today, I felt a heaviness in my chest, as if I couldn't breathe easily. Sweat trickled down from my forehead, soaking my shoulders and chest.

"I need to change quickly and prepare my heart!"
"Missionary Park, please make sure to prepare Jesus' costume well! Fighting!"
"Yes~~~"
Even though we had practiced for months, today, my role as Jesus didn't seem to connect with my heart.
"Father~~"
As I put on my costume, my heart hesitated.
A faint sound of music began to flow out, and it settled in my chest.
"What is that sound?"
I pricked up my ears and started listening carefully.

"Every night, I hide my body lower and lower, leaving to find you. I place the sorrow hidden within me into the water, walking with stealthy steps, dreaming of a baby, making my way to the well at Sychar."

'두둥실 아기!' 커다란 아가의 함박웃음이 전해져 왔다
'아기, 내 아기, 내 아들, 내 사랑하는 아이들 !!

나는 모르게 풀썩 주저 앉았다. 가슴 깊은 곳에서 무언가 쏟아져 나왔다. 생수처럼 폭포수처럼 뜨거운 눈물이!

교통사고로 떠난 사랑하는 남매와 동생 가족 다섯 명의 죽음이 떠올랐다. 낭자하게 흐르던 핏자죽, 도로에 널브러져 있던 아이들의 옷, 급하게 달리던 앰블런스 소리, 하루 아침에 맞아야 했던 청천병력 같던 생이별, 모든 게 끝난 듯 하였다.

옷을 입고 무대에 나가야 할 내가 풀썩 주저앉아 숨도 못쉬며 울고 있었다. 함께 옷을 입던 사모님들이 오셨다 나를 둘러싸고 끌어 안으며 기도해 주었다. 사랑이 밀려 왔다. 누군가를 위해 죽으신, 누군가를 위해 고통을 당하셔야 했던, 자신의 몸을 모조리 드려야 했던 그분의 사랑,

억장이 무너지는 아픔을 느끼며 함께 하던 사이, 그곳에 모인 많은 사람들의 아픔을 헤아리게 하셨다. 천천히 호흡을 가다듬고 의상을 갈아입고 무대로 나가 워십 댄스를 시작했다. 음악과 노랫말이 흘러 나왔다. 예수님 역할을 맡은 내가 두 손을 펴고 서서 관중을 바라보았다.

"A baby, my baby!"

The sound of a large child's joyful laughter reached me.
"My baby, my son, my beloved children!"

I unknowingly froze, hesitating. Something deep inside my chest poured out. Like living water, like a waterfall, hot tears flowed.The deaths of my beloved siblings and their five children, taken by a car accident, flashed before my eyes.

The gruesome sight of blood flowing, the clothes of the children scattered on the road, the frantic sound of the ambulance, the sudden, devastating separation like a thunderbolt out of the blue— it all seemed to have ended.

Dressed and ready to go on stage, I collapsed, unable to breathe, crying. The pastor's wife and others, who had been changing clothes with me, came to my side. They surrounded me, embraced me, and prayed for me. Love flooded over me. The love of the One who died for someone, who had to suffer for someone, who gave His whole body for others.

In that moment of overwhelming pain, I felt the shared suffering of those gathered there. Slowly, I calmed my breath, changed into my costume, and went on stage to begin the worship dance. The music and lyrics began to flow. As the one playing Jesus, I stood with my arms open, gazing at the audience.

"너 물가로 나오라 내 곁에 서라 네 모든 눈물 내가 씻으리라
너 어둠에 헤맬 때 흘리던 네 눈물 그 눈물을 위해 내가 죽었노라 "

물가로 나오라 워십댄스를 하는 내내 나는 눈물을 흘리며 주님의 사랑에 빠져 들었다. 주님의 핏빛 사랑이 내 사랑하는 자녀들의 영혼을 감싸고 함께 춤을 추는 것 같았다.

다른 이들을 위로하기 위해 준비한 무대가 바로 나를 위해 준비하신 주님의 비밀한 선물이었음을 알게 되었다. 많은 이들이 감동을 받은 시간이었다고 감사를 표해 왔다.

필리핀에 선교사로 떠나 오기 전, 자녀들을 잃은 슬픈 마음으로 좌절하고 낙담하여 방향을 잡지 못할 때 문화 예술 선교를 하시는 여 목사님을 통해 워십댄스를 배우게 하셨다. 몸치인 나를 워십댄스 "주만 바라볼지라"로 한 곡을 1년을 치유하시며 배우게 하셨다. 워십 댄스로 나를 치료하신 하나님께서 워십 댄스로 단기선교를 하게 하시고 상처 투성이 인 나, 너무도 부족한 것 투성이인 나를 필리핀의 선교사로 보내셨다.

"Come to the water, stand by My side. I will wash away all your tears. The tears you shed while wandering in darkness, For those tears, I died."
"Come to the water."
Throughout the worship dance, I cried and fell deeper into the love of the Lord. His crimson love seemed to envelop the souls of my beloved children, and it felt as if we were dancing together.

The stage I had prepared to comfort others turned out to be the secret gift that the Lord had prepared for me. Many people expressed their gratitude, saying it was a deeply moving experience.

Before I left for the Philippines as a missionary, I was lost in sadness, unable to find direction after losing my children. It was through a female pastor who did cultural and artistic ministry that I learned worship dance. Though I had no rhythm, she helped me heal over the course of a year with one song,
"I Will Only Look to You."
The God who healed me through worship dance then led me to use that very dance in short-term missions. Despite my wounded heart and all my shortcomings, He sent me as a missionary to the Philippines.

필리핀에서의 여러 가지 훈련과 연단 가운데 몇몇 선교사님들과 함께 문화 예술 선교의 장에 참여하게 되어 다시 워십댄스를 하게 되고 6개월 여의 준비 끝에 지난 해 10월 선교사 및 현지 사역자 150명을 초대하여 위로의 축제를 벌이게 되었다.

상처많고 넘어지기 잘하는 나를 예수님의 역할로 세우셔서 예수 역할을 통해 내가 더 은혜받고 예수님 사랑을 더 많이 나누라고 일으켜 세워 주셨다. 사역에, 삶에 지치고 넘어질 때 마다 하나님께서 주신 새 힘으로 다시 서려고 기도하며 나아간다.

나를 위해 죽으신 예수님! 그 예수님을 닮으려고 매일 몸부림 친다.

Amidst various training and trials in the Philippines, I was able to participate in cultural and artistic ministry alongside some missionaries. I began worship dancing again, and after about six months of preparation, in October of last year, I organized a comforting festival, inviting 150 missionaries and local workers.

Though I am full of wounds and often prone to falling, the Lord placed me in the role of Jesus. Through portraying Jesus, I received more grace and was encouraged to share His love even more. Every time I grew weary and stumbled in my ministry and life, I prayed and moved forward, relying on the new strength God gave me.

Jesus, who died for me! I struggle every day to become more like Him.

햇살이 놀자 하네

박혜원

햇살은 장난꾸러기
구름에 숨었다 나왔다
바람은 햇살을 찾으러
이 꽃 저 꽃 뒤집어보며
기웃거리며 찾아다니네

하루 종일 뛰어다닌 바람이
이마에 땀 닦고 한숨 돌리며
내일 또 놀자 우리
가벼운 인사하며 떠나네

줄타며 놀던 사이
얄궂은 햇살이
줄 위에 매달려 있던 빨래들을
향기로 구워 냈네

박혜원 선교사는 캐나다에 거주하면서 모슬렘 난민사역, 찬양전도 사역, 신학교 사역, 홈리스 사역을 하고 있다. 글로벌선교문학회 회원으로 활동하고 있다.

The Sun Calls to Play
by Park Hye-won

The sun, a playful sprite,
Hides and leaps from clouds' embrace,
The wind, in search of warmth,
Turns each flower over,
Peeking, searching, chasing light.

The wind, after a day of running,
Wipes sweat from its brow, sighing,
"Let's play again tomorrow,"
With a light farewell, it drifts away.

As they played and spun around,
The mischievous sun,
Baked the clothes hanging on the line,
Infusing them with a fragrant warmth.

하나님의 깜짝 선물, 우쿨렐레

박혜원

나에게 우쿨렐레는 지쳐 시냇가에 숨었던 엘리야에게 하나님께서 까마귀를 통해 공급하신 음식과도 같은 선물입니다(열왕기상 17:1-7).
전혀 예상치 못한 시점에 주신, 하나님의 두 번째 '깜짝 선물'이었습니다.
3년 전 쯤 아들의 항암 치료 차 벤쿠버에 온 장 선교사님을 돕기 위해 재능기부 교환으로 시작한 우쿨렐레가 제 인생 두 번째 깜짝 선물이 되었습니다. 단순히 위로와 재능 나눔 차원에서 시작했던 악기 하나가, 이토록 놀라운 선교의 도구가 될 줄은 그때는 몰랐습니다. 장 선교사님으로부터 몇 개월 배우고 그만둘 줄 알았는데, 지금은 벤쿠버에 두 팀, 한국에 한 팀이 결성되어 매주 거리 전도와 찬양 사역을 활발히 이어가고 있습니다.
작년, 처음으로 혼자 전도 여행을 결심했을 때 두려움과 설렘이 교차했습니다. 스페인, 포르투갈, 프랑스, 영국을 거쳐 튀르키예의 일곱 교회 유적지와 안타키아까지 이어지는 여정이었습니다. 첫 찬양 전도는 스페인 세비야 광장에서 시작됐습니다. 준비한 전도지를 이탈리아에서 온 커플에게 건넸고, 그들은 기쁘게 예수님을 영접했습니다. 그것은 하나님께서 주신 격려의 사인이었습니다.
마지막 여행지인 안타키아에서의 하루는 평생 잊지 못할 장면으로 남아 있습니다. 마지막 여행지인 안타키아(현재 안디옥)에서 근처 소도시로 버스를 타고 전도하러 떠났습니다. 버스에서 내리자마자 한국 읍 같은 분위기와 찌는 듯한 더위에 압도되었습니다.

God's Surprise Gift, The Ukulele

By Park Hye-won

To me, the ukulele is like the food that God gave Elijah through the ravens when he was tired and hiding by the stream (1 Kings 17:1-7).

It was a second "surprise gift" from God, given at a totally unexpected time. About three years ago, I started playing the ukulele to help another missionary, Pastor Jang, who came to Vancouver for his son's cancer treatment. I offered my help in exchange for a talent-sharing lesson, and that's how it all began. I never thought that this small instrument, which I started playing just for comfort and sharing, would become such a powerful tool for missions. At first, I thought I would learn for a few months and stop. But now, there are two ukulele teams in Vancouver and one in Korea. We play music and share the gospel on the streets every week.

Last year, I decided to go on my first solo mission trip. I felt both fear and excitement. The journey took me through Spain, Portugal, France, and the UK, and finally to Türkiye—visiting the ruins of the seven churches and the city of Antioch. The first street worship started in Seville, Spain. I gave a gospel flyer to a couple from Italy, and they gladly accepted Jesus. That moment was a clear sign from God—His way of encouraging me.

The last day of my mission trip, in the city of Antakya (ancient Antioch), became an unforgettable memory. On that day, I took a bus from Antakya to a small nearby town to do street evangelism.

마지막 여행지인 안타키아에서의 하루는 평생 잊지 못할 장면으로 남아 있습니다. 마지막 여행지인 안타키아(현재 안디옥)에서 근처 소도시로 버스를 타고 전도하러 떠났습니다. 버스에서 내리자마자 한국 읍 같은 분위기와 찌는 듯한 더위에 압도되었습니다. 숨이 막힐 듯한 더위 속에 우리는 함께 동네를 걸었습니다. 호텔에서부터 준비해 간 셀폰은 통역기 기능이 먹통이 되어 말도 통하지 않게 되었고, 상황은 열악했지만 성령님만 의지하며 골목길을 걸었습니다. 그리고 우연히 들어선 작은 슈퍼 앞에서 우쿨렐레를 꺼내 들었습니다.

 언어소통은 전혀 안 되었지만 악기가 소통의 가장 좋은 창구였습니다. 찬양이 시작되자, 조용하던 골목에 창문이 하나 둘 열리고 사람들이 창문 밖을 내다 보았습니다. 잠시 후 아이들과 청년들, 부인들이 몰려들기 시작했습니다. 우리는 찬양을 한 후 한 무리 보내고, 새로 온 사람들을 위해 반복해서 찬양하고 또 찬양했습니다. 미국인 권사님은 가방에서 연필 하나 꺼내 아이들 대상 게임을 진행하였습니다.

 찬양과 게임, 간식 나눔을 통해 그들은 우리에게 마음을 열었고, 우쿨렐레는 순식간에 동네의 사랑을 받은 악기가 되었습니다.

As soon as I got off the bus, I was overwhelmed by the heat and the place—it felt like a small countryside town in Korea, and the weather was extremely hot. We began walking through the village in the sweltering heat. I had prepared a phone with a translation app at the hotel, but it didn't work at all once we arrived, so we couldn't communicate with the locals. The situation wasn't easy, but we relied only on the Holy Spirit as we walked down the narrow alleys. In front of a small store we came across by chance, I took out my ukulele.

Even though we couldn't speak the same language, music became the best way to connect. As soon as the praise began, the quiet alley slowly came to life. Windows started to open one by one, and people peeked outside. Soon, children, young people, and women began to gather around us. After we finished a song, some would leave, and new people would come. We repeated the praise again and again. An American missionary woman with us pulled out a pencil from her bag and led a game for the children.

Through songs, games, and sharing snacks, people began to open their hearts to us. The ukulele quickly became the favorite sound of the neighborhood.

동리 여인들은 우리를 자기 집에 서로 초대하겠다고 빨리 가자고 졸라댔습니다. 한 집에 들어가니 시원한 에어컨 바람이 그 날의 땀과 피로를 날려주었습니다. 순박하고 사랑스런 영혼들이 음료와 맛있는 간식으로 우리를 환대해 주었습니다. 아이들은 잔뜩 호기심 어린 눈빛으로 내 우쿨렐레를 만져보고 싶어해서 허락해 주었더니 돌아가며 폼 잡고 치기 시작했습니다.

다음 날 다시 그 가정을 방문했을 때, 어제 만나지 못한 큰아들이 나타났고, "나는 무슬림인데 기독교인이 아니어도 죄 사함을 받을 수 있나요?"라고 묻는 순간, 제 심장이 멈추는 줄 알았습니다. 저는 "지금부터 내가 말하는 걸 잘 듣고 받아들인다면, 당신도 죄 사함을 받을 수 있습니다"라고 말했고, 그는 예수님을 영접했습니다. 내친김에 이 가족 모두에게 복음을 제시하고 그 청년을 위해 축복기도를 드리며 저는 분명히 알 수 있었습니다. 하나님께서 나의 전도여행을 이끄신 이유는 바로 이 청년을 만나게 하시려는 것이었음을. 우쿨렐레라는 작고 연약한 악기를 통해 하나님은 사람들의 마음을 열게 하셨고, 복음을 전할 길을 열어 주셨습니다.

하나님의 두 번째 깜짝 선물인 이 우쿨렐레는, 단순한 악기가 아니라 하나님의 능력의 도구입니다. 할렐루야!

The women in the village started urging us to hurry and visit their homes—they wanted to invite us in. When we entered one house, the cool air from the air conditioner blew away all the sweat and tiredness from the day. The kind and warm-hearted women welcomed us with drinks and delicious snacks. The children, full of curiosity, wanted to touch my ukulele. I said yes, and they took turns playing it proudly, trying to look like real musicians.

The next day, we visited the same home again. This time, their eldest son—whom we hadn't met the day before—appeared. He looked at me and asked, "I am a Muslim. Can my sins be forgiven even if I'm not a Christian?"

At that moment, my heart almost stopped. I replied, "If you listen carefully and accept what I'm about to say, then yes, your sins can be forgiven." He listened, and he accepted Jesus into his heart. After that, I shared the gospel with the whole family and prayed a blessing over the young man. At that moment, I clearly understood—this is the reason why God led me on this mission trip: to meet this young man. Through a small, simple ukulele, God opened people's hearts and made a way for the gospel to be shared.

This ukulele, God's second surprise gift for me, is not just a musical instrument—it is a powerful tool of God. Hallelujah!

나의 천국 여행기

박혜원

늘 상 고대하던 천국에 드디어 왔다. 셋째 언니가 천국 문 앞에 가서 입구에 써진 글자를 읽었다고 꿈 이야기를 했을 때부터 너무 부러운 나머지 난 언제 가보나 손꼽아 기다려왔었다. 문 앞만이 아니라 내부로 초대되어 속속히 안내 받으며 보고 싶어 얼마나 기대하며 준비했던가 새삼 기억이 떠오른다.

가장 눈에 띄는 것은 생명수가 흐르는 강이다. 그 강물의 색깔은 비치 빛과 초록 빛이 적당히 섞여 물감으로 풀어 그린 그림같이 시원하고 상큼하다. 하와이 해변가를 드라이브하며 보았던 것처럼 천국의 강물은 너무 아름다워 색깔마저 사실은 정확히 표현하기 힘들 정도로 황홀한 빛깔이다.

My Journey to Heaven
by Hye Won Park

At last, I have arrived in Heaven— the place I had longed for all my life. Ever since my third sister once shared her dream
of standing before the gates and reading the words written above, my heart has ached with wonder and yearning.

How many times did I count the days, asking quietly, "When will it be my turn?" Now I remember again the eager anticipation, the way I prepared my soul for this very moment — not merely to stand at the entrance, but to be welcomed inside, to be gently led through the wonders I had only imagined. Yet, before I follow the guided path,

And there it is — the river of the water of life. It is the first to capture my eyes and heart. The colors flow like light itself — a heavenly blend of crystal blue and soft green, like watercolor poured from the hands of God. Cool and refreshing, full of life. It reminds me of the shores of Hawaii, where the sea sparkles under the sun — but here, the beauty is unspeakably richer. Even the colors feel unearthly, as if they were never meant to be captured by words or brush. They shine with a radiance that stirs something eternal within me, leaving me breathless in awe.

옆에 세워진 조그만 보트를 타고 강줄기를 따라 둘러 보기로 했다.
　나도 모르는 사이에 주님도 보트에 타고 계셨다. "앗 주님 언제 오셨어요?" 수줍게 여쭙는 내게 주님은 살며시 웃기만 하셨다.

　'사랑하는 딸아, 그동안 수고 많았다. 네가 나로 인하여 기뻐하며 섬겨온 것, 사람을 바라보지 않고 한결같이 나만 바라보고 묵묵히 순종해 온 것, 영혼을 사랑하여 전도한 것, 불쌍한 모슬렘 난민들을 사랑으로 대해준 것, 너무 고맙다. 네 수고와 눈물, 좌절, 때로는 지치고 외로웠던 순간들 내가 다 알고 있단다.'

　'역시, 주님이셔! 어쩜 내 맘을 다 꿰뚫고 계셨지? 이 세상 누구도 나를 다 이해하고 이 정도로 격려해주고 칭찬해 준 사람은 없었지' 하는 생각이 들어 가슴이 억제할 수 없을 만큼 기뻐 뛰었다.

A small boat waited beside the river, and I stepped in, ready to drift gently along the stream of life. To my surprise, I found the Lord already there with me.

"Lord! When did You get here?" I asked, my voice laced with shy wonder. He simply smiled — a quiet, knowing smile that wrapped me in peace.

"My beloved daughter, you've labored long and well. You found joy in Me and served with a glad heart. You looked not to people for reward, but kept your eyes on Me — steady, faithful, true. You loved souls deeply, and shared My name with the lost. You showed kindness to the forgotten, even to the Muslim refugees so many chose not to see. Thank you.

I know your tears and tireless prayers. I've seen the moments you felt worn, the nights you lay awake, the times you felt alone or unseen — I was there in all of them. And my heart leapt.'

Of course⋯ it's the Lord! Who else could know my heart so perfectly? No one on earth had ever understood me like this, had ever spoken such praise or comfort with such truth. Joy rose so high within me, I felt as though I might burst with it — dancing, laughing, free.

고개를 들어 강가의 나무들을 바라보니 내가 좋아하는 초록색 중 가장 싱그럽고 귀여운 빛깔의 초록색이 다양하게 어우러져 있었다. 나무에는 잘 익은 열매들이 주렁주렁 달려있다. 하나씩 따서 몇 개를 작은 바구니에 담았다. 하나를 꺼내 맛보니 과연 온몸의 피곤이 사라지고 기분이 개운한 게 역시 치료의 나무였구나 하는 탄성이 나왔다.

강에서 내려 주님 앉아 계시던 보좌 앞으로 나아가기로 했다. 여섯 날개 달린 천사들은 날갯짓하며 찬양하고 순교자들, 먼저 올라온 성도들, 예수님의 제자들, 구약의 선지자들, 내가 알 만한 사람들도 보인다. 모두 밝고 기쁜 얼굴로 아름다운 화음을 맞춰 찬양하며 춤을 추고 있다. 나도 모르게 리듬에 맞춰 찬양하며 몸을 흔든다.

I lifted my gaze toward the trees lining the riverbank. Their leaves shimmered in the loveliest shades of green — each hue more vivid, more cheerful, than any green I had ever seen on earth. It was as if all my favorite tones of green had gathered here in perfect harmony. The branches were heavy with fruit, ripe and glowing with life. I reached up and gently picked a few, placing them in a small basket I found nearby. Then I took one, brought it to my lips, and tasted heaven.

I whispered, tears brimming. I stepped off the boat and made my way toward the throne where the Lord had been sitting. Angels with six wings soared above, their wings shimmering with light as they moved in praise. Their voices rose like a river of song, joining with the martyrs, the saints who had gone before, the disciples of Jesus, the prophets of old —and even familiar faces I recognized, all gathered in perfect harmony. Their expressions were radiant with joy, their eyes full of light. They danced and sang, each note a thread in a tapestry of divine worship. The music swelled around me, and without even realizing it, my body began to sway, my lips joined in the song, caught up in the rhythm of heaven.

보좌 옆 네 생물을 보면서 미처 다 이해되지 않았던 부분들을 주님께 직접 물어봤다. '아 그랬구나 역시 주님이셔'하는 마음이 들었다. 허다한 무리의 성도들이 구별되어 모여 있었는데 모두 한 마음으로, 한 목소리와 한 영으로 주님을 찬양하며 경배하는데 너무 아름다워 말로 표현할 수 없을 지경이었다.

'이것이야 말로 말로만 듣고 상상했던 천상의 예배구나'라는 실감이 났다. 주님 앞에 성도들과 함께 모여 예배드리니 너무 기쁘고 내 영이 더욱 살아나니 시간 가는 줄 모를 지경이었다.

마침 그때 주님이 보낸 천사가 내게 다가와 이제 떠날 시간임을 알려준다. 이 천사가 주님이 내게 하신 말을 속삭이며 전해주었다. '이제 다시 세상에 돌아가 인내하며 순종하며 내 사명을 다하고 다시 오라'고….

Standing near the throne, I gazed at the four living creatures, full of wonder at their mystery. There were things I had never fully understood — but now, face to face with the Lord, I asked Him directly. And with each answer, my heart nodded in awe — Ah, I see now… of course, Lord. Only You could reveal such truth with such grace. Before me, an uncountable multitude of saints had gathered. They stood not in confusion, but in perfect unity — one heart, one voice, one Spirit — lifting up praise and worship to the Lamb. It was so breathtaking, so glorious, that words could never do it justice. It was the heavenly worship

I had only ever imagined in whispers and dreams. Here, at last, I knew: This is real. This is the worship of eternity. To stand with the saints before the throne, to worship my Lord face to face — it filled me with such joy, such renewal, that I lost all sense of time.

Then, quietly, a soft light approached me — an angel sent by the Lord. He came close and gently spoke:

"It's time to return now." And leaning in, he whispered the words of the Lord into my soul: "Go back to the world once more. Endure with patience. Walk in obedience. Fulfill the calling I have placed within you. And then… return to Me."

동인작가글

동행
이미셀

홀로 걷던 길 찬서리 내리면
수 겹옷 여미며 걷다 서고
웃다 울며 당신께 속삭였지요

춤추는 천사의 날개짓에
그려지는 따뜻한 유월 하늘
가슴 물들이며 불태우던 황금빛 노을 속
애태우며 설레임으로 기다렸지요

무정한 폭풍우 몰아치고
사나운 짐승에 생채기 났지만
하나뿐인 아들 떠나보낸 사라처럼
담담한 여인이 되었어요

이미셀님은 Denturist (의치사)로 11년째 활동하며 캐나다 서부 Port Hardy 땅을 섬기고 있습니다. 캐나다 선교사들을 도와 원주민사역에 기여하고 있다. 글로벌선교문학회 회원으로 활동 중이다.

Companion

by Michelle Lee

When frost settled on the path I walked alone,
I pulled my coat tight, pausing, whispering to you
laughing, weeping, all the same.

The angels' wings painted the skies of June,
a warmth that stained my heart,
as golden flames of sunset burned,
and longing swelled within me,
waiting, trembling, hoping.
Then came the ruthless storm,
the beasts that clawed and tore.
Yet like Sarah, who bid farewell to her only son,
I became a woman of quiet resolve.

아련히 애태우는 가을 냄새
노랑 빨강 은빛을 내며
떠나는 나무와 숲
사랑했어요 이젠 안녕

은발처럼 머릿발 희어지는 나이
사랑하지 못한 순간 떠오르면
자작나무처럼 떨리는 가슴으로
당신 품 파고들며 두 손 모으지요

The wistful scent of autumn lingers,
as trees and forests, cloaked in gold, crimson, and silver,
bid their quiet farewell.
I loved them once—now, I let them go.

Like silver strands in aging hair,
memories of love left unspoken rise within me.
With a trembling heart,
like a birch swaying in the wind,
I fold my hands and rest in your embrace.

Northern Island Life

Michelle Lee

   고요하고 한적한 이곳에서 나를 돌아본다. 시끄럽고 복잡한 인간관계에 가려 보이지 않게 되던 자연 만물을 오롯이 혼자 느껴본다. 하늘과 바람과 나무들과 물소리 사이에 나지막히 서서 거닐고 있다

   숲의 향기와 신선한 공기로 둘러싸인 나는 하늘 향해 춤추는 나무들이 빚어내는 Northern Island 하늘가를 쳐다보며 영혼의 포구같은 아늑함을 느낀다. 엄마의 품에 안긴 아가처럼 포근함을 느끼며 나를 이끄는 무엇에 끌려 긴 여행을 시작한다.

   눈을 감고 호흡을 한다. 깊이 숨을 들이쉴 때 차오르는 이 충만함. 온 몸에 자연의 충만함이 흐르는 걸 느낀다. 후우 하고 내쉬니 웅크리고 있던 상처와 찌꺼기가 녹아 사라진다. 두 손을 뻗어 춤을 춘다. 손끝에 영의 호흡을 담아 기쁨을 노래한다. 숲을 찾은 요정들을 위해 깔린 연두색 이끼를 밟으며 지나가는데 각종 버섯들과 식물들이 숨은 그림처럼 나타나 마음을 빼앗는다. 쓰러져 오래 잠든 고목은 제 속을 비워내고 많은 짐승들의 집이 되어준다. 코요테의 집이 아닐까 생각하며 부지런히 걷는다. 요정처럼 끝없이 춤추며 걷는 내게 나무잎 사이에 걸린 햇살 튀어나오며 '이젠 안녕' 속삭여 준다.

Northern Island Life

by Michelle Lee

In this quiet and serene place, I turn inward. Here, away from the noise and tangled threads of human affairs, I finally see nature as it is—pure, unfiltered. I stand still, then walk softly,
wrapped in the hush of sky, wind, trees, and flowing water.

Surrounded by the fresh breath of the forest, I gaze upon the Northern Island sky, where trees sway like dancers, reaching for heaven. A deep comfort settles over me— like a child cradled in a mother's arms. Drawn by something unseen, I surrender to the quiet call of a long journey.

I close my eyes and breathe in. As my lungs fill, so does my spirit— a fullness that courses through me, the very essence of nature itself. I exhale, releasing burdens long held within, melting away the shadows of old wounds. Stretching my arms, I dance,
fingertips tracing the rhythm of the spirit's breath, singing joy into the air. As I step across the moss—soft and green, laid out like a carpet for visiting fairies— hidden wonders emerge.
Mushrooms and tiny plants, delicate as whispers, steal my heart.
An ancient tree, long fallen and hollowed with time, has become a home for woodland creatures. Perhaps a coyote dwells within?
With that thought, I press on, dancing my way forward like a wandering sprite. The golden sun, slipping through the leaves,
catches my face and whispers, "Farewell, for now."

줄지어 둘러싼 삼나무와 자작나무들의 인사를 받으며 발을 옮긴다. 집에 돌아와 잠시 기도를 하고 자리에 눕는다. 고요한 평강의 강가로 잦아들며 내 영은 밤하늘 별들을 지난다. 별들의 노래를 들으며 지구를 내려다 본다. 저 바닷속 고래의 노랫소리가 별들과 하나 되어 하나님을 찬미하는 소리를 듣는다.

한밤중이지만 가끔 의식이 깨어나면 불을 켜지 않고 커텐을 활짝 연다. 기대어 앉아 커다란 창너머 밤하늘을 본다. 하늘 아래 짙은 숲의 실루엣과 그 위로 떨어지는 별빛이 성큼 걸어 들어온다. 저기 저 유독 환하게 쏟아지는 저 빛은 무엇일까?

지면에서 떠오를 때 가장 크고 환한 달, 달이 서서히 나무들 사이로 멀어져 사라질 때까지도 호기심 가득한 눈빛을 거둘 수 없다. 만물을 다스렸던 태초의 아담처럼 하나님께서 내게 베푸시고 내 앞에 두신 만물들을 마음으로 쓰다듬고 만지며 격려하듯 속삭인다. 조금만 더 기다려, 이제 곧 하나님의 아들들이 나타나서 너희들을 해방시켜 줄거야 (롬 8:19-22)라고.

Welcomed by rows of towering cedars and slender birch trees, I step forward, their silent greetings rustling in the breeze. Back home, I pause for a prayer, then lie down. As I drift toward the quiet river of peace, my soul sails beyond the stars of the night sky. From above, I gaze upon the earth, listening to the song of the stars. Somewhere in the deep ocean, a whale sings, its melody rising to join the celestial chorus, a hymn of praise to God.

Though it is the middle of the night, I sometimes wake, my spirit stirring. Without turning on a light, I pull back the curtains, settling by the window to take in the night sky. The dense forest below stands in dark silhouette, while stardust spills down in golden cascades. But what is that? That one, dazzling beyond the rest—what could it be?

The moon, at its grandest just as it rises from the earth, slowly drifts beyond the trees, yet my eyes remain fixed in wonder. Like Adam in the beginning, entrusted with the care of all living things, I reach out—not with hands, but with my heart—tracing the quiet presence of creation. Softly, I whisper to me,

"Hold on just a little longer… Soon, the sons of God will come, and you will be set free." (Romans 8:19-22)

신이 주신 자연의 품속에 살며 인간으로서의 정체성에 대해 질문하게 된다. 편리함과 신속함과 발전과 결과를 요구하기 위해 만들어진 AI가 영적인 존재로서의 인간을 어찌 다 이해하고 흉내낼까? 화려한 도심속의 인간은 차가운 AI를 닮아가는 것 아닐까? 화려한 불빛을 뿜어내던 소돔 고모라 성의 인간들은 매일 무엇을 꿈꾸며 살았을까?

　　인간다움은 무엇인가? 기다릴 줄 알고 고뇌하며 슬퍼할 줄 알고 이해하고 용서하며 긍휼히 여길 줄 아는 것, 인내하며 수고하여 얻은 열매의 단맛을 아는 것, 나를 만드신 창조주를 끝없이 갈망하고 그분의 뜻을 찾아 구하는 것이 아닐까? 나는 지구 어디쯤에 서서 무엇을 추가하고 있는 것일까?

　　긴 사유의 언덕을 지나 영혼의 자유함을 느끼며 하나님 영안에 있는 나를 보는 듯 하다. 어느 새 Northern Island 숲속 새들의 목소리와 춤추던 나뭇가지처럼 온몸으로 기뻐하며 그 분을 경배드린다.

Living in the embrace of nature, a gift from God,
I find myself questioning what it truly means to be human.

How could AI—created for speed, convenience, progress, and results— ever grasp the depths of a soul? Could it mimic the spiritual essence of a being formed by the breath of God? And in the dazzling cities, are people not slowly becoming more like the cold intelligence they created? What dreams filled the hearts of those in Sodom and Gomorrah, as they lived beneath their glittering lights?

What does it mean to be truly human? To know how to wait, to wrestle with sorrow, to understand, forgive, and show mercy. To taste the sweetness of labor's fruit, earned through patience and toil. To long endlessly for the Creator, seeking His will with every breath. Where do I stand on this vast earth, and what is it that my soul aches for?

Through the long hills of contemplation, I step into a deeper freedom— a sense of belonging within the spirit of God. Like the birds of the Northern Island forest, like the swaying trees that dance in the wind, my whole being rejoices, lifting up a song of worship to Him.

원주민과 Denturist

미셸 리

후두둑 내리던 봄비가 잦아들고 있다. 빗물은 지붕에서 떨어져 졸졸 소리를 내며 잔디밭으로 흩어진다. 이곳은 겨울비가 많이 내린다. 여름은 화창하니 모두가 기다리는 계절이다. 이런저런 계절 이야기를 하며 반갑게 덴쳐 환자들을 만나는 나는 덴쳐리스트이다.

꿈에서 빙하를 구경하는 크루즈선에서 치과 환자들을 만나고 있던 나는 밴쿠버 아일랜드에서 가장 북쪽끝에 있는 Port Hardy 란 곳에 오게 되었다. 어릴때부터 손재주가 남달랐던 나는 이곳 캐나다에서 덴쳐리스트에 도전했고 하나님께서는 그 길을 열어주셨다. 그리고 남편의 비즈니스를 따라와 덴쳐클리닉을 열게 되었다.

틀니를 맞추려면 5회 정도의 클리닉 방문이 있어야 한다. 전문 병원이나 편의 시설과 멀리 떨어진 Port Hardy에 사는 주민들은 틀니를 해넣기 위해 두시간이나 떨어진 먼 도시까지 가야했다. 그래서 Port Hardy 뿐 아니라 근처 작은 섬들과 마을에 흩어져 사는 환자들이 텐쳐클리닉이 생긴 것을 고마워 하며 찾아왔다. 그러나 몸이 불편하거나 차가 없어 그마저도 못오는 환자들에게는 내가 찾아가는 서비스를 해주었다.

The Denturist and the Indigenous Community
By Michelle Lee

The spring rain that once fell in steady streams is now quieting down. Droplets trickle from the roof, whispering gently as they scatter across the lawn. Here, the winters are long and wet, but summer is bright and beautiful—an eagerly awaited season for all. As a denturist, I greet each patient warmly, often exchanging stories about the weather and the changing seasons.

I once dreamed of treating dental patients aboard a cruise ship sailing past glacial landscapes. That dream, in a way, brought me to Port Hardy—the northernmost tip of Vancouver Island. Since childhood, I've been gifted with skilled hands. That gift led me to pursue a career as a denturist here in Canada, and by God's grace, doors opened for me. Following my husband's business path, I was given the opportunity to establish a denture clinic of my own.

Port Hardy, remote from specialist care and public facilities, has limited access to transportation and healthcare. For residents here, receiving dentures often requires five or more home visits from a mobile denture clinic like mine. This need draws not only the people of Port Hardy, but also those from neighboring islands and small communities who seek my care and expertise.

캐나다는 마약 때문에 이십 대에 벌써 모든 치아를 잃고 덴쳐를 하는 환자들이 늘고 있다. 원주민들의 마약중독으로 인한 실태는 더욱 심각하다. 거의 매주 젊은 십 대부터 삼사십대에 이르기까지 마약을 하다 목숨을 잃거나 자살로 이 세상을 떠나버렸다. 그런 이야기를 들으면 마음이 아파 탄식하며 기도한다.

"주여, 이 땅을 고쳐주소서. 마약과 술이 아닌 말씀과 성령술에 취하게 하소서. 저들로 하나님 자녀로서의 정체성이 세워져 소망을 갖고 살게 하소서"

"미셀, 나에게 헐리웃 여배우처럼 예쁜 이빨을 만들어줘." 4년 전 처음 치료를 시작하는 날, Lily 할머니는 유독 아름답고 큰 눈을 반짝이며 말씀하셨다. Lily 할머니로부터 처음 진료 상담전화를 받았을때는 도통 무슨 말을 하는지 몰라 헤메었다. 70이 넘으신 Lily 할머니는 영어보다는 원주민 고유어를 더 편하게 쓰시는 분이셨던 것이다. 9명의 형제 자매가 있었는데 그 중 두 분이 기숙학교 생존자라고 했다. 그 악명높은 원주민 학교에서는 말 안 듣는다고 아이들의 생이빨을 뽑았다고 했다. 그럴 때마다 그들을 위해 주께 엎드리며 나아간다.

Lily 할머니는 클리닉에 올 수 없는 처지여서 방문서비스를 해주었다. 그러면서 Lily 할머니 집을 참 많이 드나들었다. 여러 장비와 재료를 챙겨 가야하기에 쉬운 일은 아니었지만 환자와 친밀감을 쌓아갈 수 있었다. Lily 할머니는 카치노 마을밴드에 사신다. 수풀이 양 옆으로 우거진 쭉 뻗은 시골 도로를 15분 정도 달리는 거리에 카치노밴드가 있다.

In Canada, it is becoming increasingly common for patients in their twenties to lose all their teeth due to drug use and require full dentures. Among Indigenous communities, the crisis is even more severe. Week after week, I hear of lives lost—young teens to men and women in their thirties and forties—taken by drug overdoses or suicide. My heart aches with every story, and I can only sigh and pray:

"Lord, heal this land. Let them be filled not with substances, but with Your Word and the wine of the Holy Spirit. Let them know who they are as children of God, and live with hope restored."

"I want teeth like a Hollywood movie star, Michelle," said Grandma Lily on the first day we began her treatment four years ago. Her large, beautiful eyes sparkled as she spoke. I still remember the first phone call I received from her. I could barely understand what she was saying. At over 70 years old, Grandma Lily was far more comfortable speaking her Indigenous language than English.

She told me she had nine siblings, two of whom were survivors of the residential school system. She shared how, at those notorious institutions, children had their teeth pulled out simply for not obeying. Every time I hear such stories, I find myself again on my knees, praying for them before the Lord.

Sometimes I offer mobile denture services, visiting patients who are unable to come to the clinic. It's no easy task—there's equipment, materials, and careful preparation involved. One home I visited frequently was Grandma Lily's. She lives in the Cachino Band in the small community of Cachino. It's about a fifteen-minute drive down a long country road, flanked by thick forest on both sides.

지난달 Lily 할머니는 수줍은 다섯 살 같은 남동생 Stanley을 데리고 왔다. Stanley 도 Lily 할머니처럼 결혼을 해 본적 없이 혼자 산다. 언제부터 이가 없었는지 이가 다 빠지고도 틀니를 하지 않아서 잇몸이 다 닳아져 가고 있었다. 이전에 치과에서 틀니를 만들어 다녔는데 무슨 일인지 중간에 치료를 중단하게 되었다고 했다. 나는 그의 덴쳐를 무사히 잘 맞춰 끼웠고 그는 드디어 멋진 미소를 가진 훈남으로 다시 태어났다.

원주민들을 위해 덴쳐리스트의 발길을 옮길 때마다 좌우를 분별하지 못하는 니느웨 백성을 아끼신 하나님께서 저들도 사랑하시고 돌보시는 보호자가 되어 주시는 것 같습니다. 웬지 이들이 내게 맡겨진 연약한 아기들 같아 그 영혼을 품고 더 사랑해야지 하는 생각을 합니다. 환자를 보는 나의 얼굴에서 하나님의 사랑과 생명의 빛이 뿜어져 나와 그들에게 비춰어져서 그들 또한 예수 생명안으로 가득 채워지기를 기도합니다.

"주여, 이들 원주민들에게 채워진 어둠의 족쇄가 끊기고 만물을 충만케 하시는 예수님안에 들어와 자유와 평강과 기쁨을 누릴 수 있게 하소서. 이 캐나다 서부 밴쿠버섬 북쪽끝에 자리잡은 원주민 마을로부터 성령의 바람이 크게 불어 캐나다 전역 원주민마을로 번지어 하나님 나라가 세워지고 그 분께서 통치하실 날이 곧 오게 하소서 주여 !"

Last month, Grandma Lily brought along her shy younger brother, Stanley—like a five-year-old in a grown man's body. Like his sister, Stanley has never married and has lived alone all his life. No one could say exactly when he lost his teeth, but he had gone without dentures for so long that his gums were severely worn down. He mentioned that he had once started treatment for dentures but, for some reason, never completed it. I was able to fit him with a new set of dentures, and by God's grace, they were a perfect fit. That day, Stanley was reborn—a fine gentleman with a bright and confident smile.

Each time I travel as a denturist to serve the Indigenous people, I am reminded of the God who showed compassion to the people of Nineveh, who could not tell their right hand from their left. I sense that God, too, is the protector of these people, deeply loving and caring for them. Somehow, I see them as fragile little children entrusted to me—precious souls to be embraced with even greater love. I pray that the love and light of God would radiate from my face as I treat them, and that they would be filled with the life of Jesus through every smile we restore.

"Lord, break the chains of darkness that hold the hearts of these Indigenous people. Bring them into the fullness of Christ—into freedom, peace, and true joy. From this remote Indigenous village at the northern tip of Vancouver Island, may a mighty wind of the Holy Spirit rise and sweep across Indigenous communities throughout Canada. Establish Your kingdom, O Lord, and reign over this land!"

벚꽃 엔딩
이정희

목련이 질 때를 기다려
하얀 미소를 날리던 그와 같이
벚꽃이 봄 하늘을 가득 채웠다

바람만 불어도 돌아서는 줄 알면서도
오늘은 구름까지 데려와 속삭이더니
내귀에 비창곡을 들려 주었다.

매화 꽃이 지면 매실이 열리고
이별이 떠나면 설레임이 다가오듯
벚꽃이 지면 버찌를 따 먹을 양
시린 마음을 달래며 걷는다

나즉히 고개 떨구고 향기 피워내는
너를 맨발로 밟으며 콧노래로 걸을 때
오랜 그리움이 살포시 가슴에 앉는다.

이정희 선교사는 학창시절 CCC에서 캠퍼스 복음화에 열정을 품다. 러시아 세인트피터스버그에서 28년 사역후 한국에서 남편 김도수 목사와 성화 전시 사역 중. 글로벌선교문학회 회원으로 활동 중이다.

Cherry Blossom Ending
by Lee Jeonghee

I waited for the magnolias to fall,
as he once did—sending white smiles through the breeze.
Now the cherry blossoms have filled the spring sky,
soft as sighs, light as his touch.

Though I knew the petals would turn at the slightest wind,
today, he brought even the clouds to whisper with me—
a murmur so tender, it played
a song of sorrow in my ear.

When plum blossoms fade, green plums begin to grow;
when goodbyes depart, new heartbeats draw near.
As the cherry trees let go their blooms,
I walk on—cool heart calmed
by the promise of ripening cherries.

When I tread gently on fallen scent,
barefoot, humming without thought,
something old and quietly aching
comes to rest within my chest—
a longing, blooming once more.

러시아를 위한 기도

이정희

황량한 들판 위에 총성이 멈추기를
상처 입은 영혼마다 주의 손길 닿기를
검은 구름 헤치고 평화의 빛 비추사,
그리스도의 사랑으로 저 땅을 감싸주소서.

분열과 증오 속에 진리가 잊혀졌으나,
십자가의 능력으로 굳은 마음 여시고,
용서의 언어가 총알을 대신하게 하므로
회복의 강물 흐르게 인도하여 주소서.

토스도엡스키의 혼이 피어나던 시절처럼,
깊은 사유와 아름다움이 다시 피어나
시와 음악, 붓과 사랑 넘치게 하시고
성령의 숨결로 문화의 불을 지펴 주소서.

무너진 벽 너머로 형제가 서로를 껴안고,
주 안에서 하나 되어 새날을 노래하므로
황폐한 땅에 하늘 찬미 소리 퍼지게 하시며
고통을 지나 소망을 품고 일어나게 하소서.

A Prayer for Russia
by Lee Jeonghee

Let gunfire cease on barren plains so wide,
Let healing hands touch every soul that cried.
Break through the clouds with peace like morning light,
And wrap that land in Christ's embracing might.

Though truth lies lost in hatred's darkened reign,
Unseal the hearts through cross-borne love and pain.
Let words of pardon silence war's cruel sound,
Till streams of healing flood the broken ground.

As once when Dostoevsky's soul took flight,
Let thought and beauty blossom into light.
With song and brush, with pen and holy flame,
Revive the arts that glorify Your name.

Beyond the walls where brothers once stood torn,
Let unity in Christ anew be born.
Let praise arise where desolation lay,
And hope take root to bloom from grief's decay.

동인작가글

러시아에서 만난 평양 손님

이정희

푸쉬킨과 토스토엡스키가 살았다는 이유만으로도 내가 산 러시아 피터스버그는 낯설지 않다. 끝날 것 같지 않은 춥고도 긴긴 겨울엔 하루 종일 검은 빌오드 같은 어둠을 휘감고 산다.

오렌지 향이 나는 홍차를 흡족히 마시며 석 달 내내 내리는 눈에 털모자를 깊이 쓴 닥터 지바고가 생각날 무렵 모스코바에서 귀한 손님 몇이 찾아 와 주었다. 손님이 들려주던 깊고 뜨거운 감동의 이야기를 전하려 한다. 그중에 여든세 살의 김선혁 씨가 계셨다. 마치 다윗의 향취가 배어나는 분이셨는데 내게 귀한 책을 선물로 주셨고, 나는 커다란 감동과 도전을 받았다. 그분의 이름은 김선혁, 수많은 어려움과 고통, 핍박 중에도 신앙을 지키며 국가를 위해 투쟁해 온 그분의 생생한 삶의 여정을 나누려 한다.

김선혁 선생님은 "평양에서 서울까지 47년"이란 책을 선물로 준 저자였다. 그는 평양에서 태어나고 아버지는 산정현교회 장로이자 평양의 실업가이며 김일성의 친구였고 조만식 선생과도 깊은 관계였다.

A Guest from Pyongyang, Met in Russia
by Lee Jeonghee

I chose to live in Russia, simply because it was the land of Pushkin and Dostoevsky. And so, Saint Petersburg never felt unfamiliar to me. Through winters that seemed to have no end— cold and endlessly long— I wrapped myself in a darkness like a black billboard that hung in the sky all day long.

With a cup of orange-scented black tea warming my hands, as snow quietly fell for three months without rest, my thoughts would wander to Doctor Zhivago, buried deep in his fur hat,

moving through the silent streets of Moscow. It was in such a season that a few precious guests came to visit me from that city. They brought with them stories—deep and burning with emotion— and I feel compelled now to share them. Among them was an 83-year-old gentleman named Kim Sun-hyuk. There was something of David's fragrance about him— a quiet nobility, a strength shaped by suffering. He gave me a treasured book, and I, in turn, received a deep stirring in my soul. His name is Kim Sun-hyuk, a man who preserved his faith through countless trials, and who carried his conviction for his country like a banner through persecution and pain.

The book he gifted me was titled "Forty-Seven Years from Pyongyang to Seoul." Born in Pyongyang, he was the son of a businessman and an elder of Sanjeonghyeon Church. His father had once been a friend of Kim Il-sung, and also shared deep ties with the revered Jo Man-sik.

열네 살, 중학교 어린 나이에 일본의 압제에서 벗어나자 그는, 러시아의 "신탁통치 반대"를 외쳤다.
그 후 친구들과 감옥에 갇혀 짐승처럼 러시아 이곳저곳을 끌려다니며 고통당하던 중, 많은 벗을 잃었다.

마지막에 끌려간 곳이 유배지 시베리아 였다. 그곳에서 십 년의 옥고 후 출옥했으나 정치범이라는 이유로 감옥에서 벗어나지 못하고 겨울엔 영하 40도 바닥에 널판지 가마니를 덮고 잤다. 고아인 러시아 여인과 결혼 하여 첫 아이는 얼어서 병에 걸려 죽었다 한다. 이렇게 북한에서 정치범으로 끌려온 사람들이 20만 명이나 된다고 전해주었다.

그는 항상 아버지의 믿음을 본받아 신앙으로 살며 성실하게 일하고 선한 일을 하며 살려 했고 가족과 어머니를 그리워 많이 울었다. 악명 높은 스탈린이 죽고 가족들은 모두 남한으로 이동했다. 어머니는 자녀들이 용돈을 드려도 안 쓰시고 막내 아들 선혁이 오면 주겠다며 꼭꼭 모으셨다 한다.

At the tender age of fourteen, still only a middle school student, he raised his voice against Soviet trusteeship, just as Korea was breaking free from Japan's grip. That bold cry led to prison— where he and his friends were dragged like beasts from one place to another across the vastness of Russia.

Many of those dear friends never made it out. The final place he was taken to was exile—Siberia. There, he endured ten long years of imprisonment. Even after release, his label as a political criminal kept him locked in yet another kind of prison. In the brutal winters, where the air dropped to forty degrees below zero, he lay on the frozen ground with only a plank and a burlap sack for warmth. He later married a Russian woman, an orphan herself. Their first child, born into the cold, became ill and died. He told me there were as many as 200,000 like him— people who had been taken as political prisoners from North Korea.

Yet through it all, he tried to live by the faith of his father. With quiet resolve, he worked hard, lived honestly, and did what good he could, even in a land that had forgotten compassion. He wept often—for his mother, for his family, for home. When the notorious Stalin died, his family was finally allowed to move to South Korea. His mother, even in her old age, would save the small allowances her daughters gave her, saying, "I'll give this to Sun-hyuk when he returns." She tucked them away carefully, waiting, always waiting.

미국으로 시집간 여동생이 날마다 막내 아들을 그리워하며 우시는 어머니를 위해 구소련이 무너지자 시베리아 고려인협회를 통해 선혁씨를 찾게 되었다. 헤어진 지 47년 만에 수속을 밟아 김포공항에서 식구들과 재회를 했고 그 광경을 지켜보던 공항의 모든 이들이 함께 울며 감동의 시간을 가졌다 한다.

　오랜 시간 어머니의 품에 안겨 울던 선혁씨가 어머니에게 말했다.
"어머니, 47년 동안 못 본 막내 아들 선혁이예요."
"47 년이라구? 아들아 나는 날마다 꿈에서 보았단다?"

　어머니와 함께 집에서 며칠을 묵었는데, 어느 날 치매 증상인 어머니가 그를 보며 가족에게 물었다 한다.
"저 손님은 왜 안가고 우리 집에서 계속 계시니.?"

　김선혁씨의 어머니가 돌아가시기 전 쓰신 짧은 편지가 읽는 이들의 가슴을 울렸다 한다.

After the collapse of the former Soviet Union, his younger sister—now living in the United States— could no longer bear to watch their mother weep each day, longing for her youngest son. Through the Korean Association in Siberia, they began searching for Sun-hyuk. After 47 long years of separation, he completed the necessary paperwork and finally reunited with his family at Gimpo Airport. It is said that everyone who witnessed the moment wept together, touched deeply by the beauty and pain of that long-awaited embrace.

As Sun-hyuk sobbed in his mother's arms, he gently whispered,

"Mother… it's me, your youngest son, Sun-hyuk. I haven't seen you in 47 years."

To which his mother, still holding him tightly, replied,

"Forty-seven years, you say? But my son, I saw you every day… in my dreams."

He stayed with her for a few days, basking in the warmth of home. But one day, as signs of dementia began to cloud her mind, she turned to the family and asked softly,

"Why is that guest still here… and not leaving our house?"

Before she passed away, Sun-hyuk's mother left behind a short, handwritten letter. Those who read it said it moved them to tears.

"보고 싶은 아들 선혁아! 나는 건강하게 잘 있다. 하나님이 우리나라를 통일시켜 주시면 너도 와서 함께 평양에 가서 살자"

김선혁 씨는 그 후 러시아로 돌아가 생사를 모르는 친구들의 상황을 찾아 부모들에게 75명의 소식을 알려주는 일을 했다.

한밤의 전설 같은 평양 손님의 이야기로 가슴에 눈물이 흐르고 창밖의 눈도 지나간 아픔을 땅바닥에 쏟아놓으며 함께 한다.

세월이 가고 통일의 기도가 쌓이면 봄이 오듯 아픔도 녹고 통일의 무궁화가 삼천리금수강산에 만발하고 용서와 화해의 강물이 온 땅을 치유할 꿈을 꾸어 본다.

"My beloved son, Sun-hyuk, whom I long to see—
I am well and in good health.
If God grants us the gift of reunification,
let us go together and live once more in Pyongyang."

After that, Kim Sun-hyuk returned to Russia. There, he devoted himself to tracing the lives of friends whose fates remained unknown. Through his efforts, he was able to deliver news of seventy-five such people to their long-waiting families.

His story—like a legend whispered at midnight—left tears upon my heart. Outside the window, the falling snow seemed to grieve too,
spilling the sorrows of the past softly onto the earth.

As time flows on and prayers for reunification gather like blossoms, perhaps, like the return of spring, our wounds will thaw. Perhaps the mugunghwa—the rose of Sharon—will bloom again across the land from sea to sea. And perhaps the river of forgiveness and reconciliation will rise and heal this nation, every corner of it, with a dream we still dare to dream.

동인작가 글

어떤 길

이진종

좌, 우
어느 길을 택해야 할까
선택의 기로에서
때로는 침묵으로
때로는 롯처럼 주저한다
좁은 길이 정답일까
아무도 말해주지 않는
그 길을 가야만 할까

변수가 많다
위험부담도 크다
생각이 많아진다
정답도 모른 채
지나온 흔적
지나친 조바심이 장애물이다.
일단 믿어보자
한 발을 내 딛는다.

이진종 시인, 목사는 199년 캐나다 이민 후 "캘거리 문협" 수필 부문 신춘문예 등단 하면서 문단에 나옴. 2014년 "한비문학" 시부문 등단, 캘거리 한인문인협회 회장을 역임했으며 캘거리 코스타 대표 역임. 현재 원주민 선교와 시리아 난민 사역중. 저서로는 "세상을 보는 눈" 외 2권이 있다.

A Certain Path

by Jin-jong Lee

Left or right,
which road should I take?
At the crossroads of choice,
sometimes in silence,
sometimes hesitating—like Lot.
Is the narrow path the right one?
Must I walk it,
though no one tells me so?

Too many variables,
too great a risk.
Thoughts multiply,
yet the answer remains unknown.
Traces of the past,
restless impatience—obstacles in my way.
But for now, I choose to trust.
I take a step forward.

구십구도

이진종

'섭씨 99 도'라는 책에서 주인공 올리버가 자전거를 타고 가다 트럭과 부딪혀 사고를 당한다. 이후 자신감을 잃고 사람들과 격리된 채 살아간다. 말조차 잃어버린다. 그러다 우연히 만난 사람들과 교제를 통해 소통하게 됨은 물론 자신감을 회복하고 자신의 재능을 발견하게 된다는 내용이다.

가난과 아픔과 상실 등 부친 사업의 실패, 서른 두 살 아내의 죽음 등 자신의 삶을 시로 토해 내어 유명해진 도종환의 시인은 '흔들리며 피는 꽃'에서 흔들리며 곧게 세우는 아름다움을 표현한다.

"흔들리지 않고 피는 꽃이 어디 있으랴
이 세상 그 어떤 아름다운 꽃들도
흔들리며 피었나니
흔들리면서 줄기를 곧게 세웠나니
흔들리지 않고 가는 사랑이 어디 있으랴

젖지 않고 피는 꽃이 어디 있으랴
이 세상 그 어떤 빛나는 꽃들도
다 젖으며 피었나니
바람과 비에 젖으며 꽃잎 따뜻하게 피웠나니
젖지 않고 가는 삶이 어디 있으랴"

Ninety-Nine Degrees
by Lee Jin-jong

In the book '99 Degrees Celsius', the protagonist Oliver crashes into a truck while riding his bicycle. Wounded, he retreats from the world— losing his words, losing his will. But through divine providence, he meets strangers who become bridges: through fellowship, he rediscovers his voice, his confidence, his gift.

Poet Do Jong-hwan, whose life was marred by poverty, grief, the collapse of his father's business, and the passing of his wife at thirty-two, poured his sorrow into poetry. In The Flower That Blooms While Swaying, he speaks of the beauty born from brokenness:

"What flower blooms without trembling?
All the beautiful blossoms in this world
have swayed as they bloomed.
They stood upright, even as they shook.
What love endures without being shaken?

What flower blooms without being soaked?
All the radiant blossoms in this world
bloomed wet—petals warmed by wind and rain.
What life endures without being soaked?"

Yes— faith, like the flower, blooms not in stillness, but in struggle. And perhaps, ninety-nine degrees is not the end, but the holy threshold before the final boiling point of transformation.

아픈 만큼 성숙해지는 법이다. 시인이 한 편의 시를 발표하기 위해서는 적어도 100편의 시를 완성해야 하고, 천 편의 시를 습작해야 하고, 만 편의 시를 읽어야 한다고 한다. 김난도는 천 번을 흔들려야 어른이 된다고 했다.

누구나 핸디캡을 갖고 있다. 나도 어릴 적에, 친 할아버지가 돌아가신 날에 앞니가 빠졌다. 그런데 우연하게도 새로 난 이가 검은색이었다. 그 뒤로 사람들 앞에서 잘 웃지도 않았고, 입을 벌리지도 않았다.

어느 날, 교회에서 교사로 봉사할 때였다. 치과에 근무하고 있었던 한 분이 내 치아를 보더니 말했다.
"선생님, 언제부터 치아가 이랬나요? 이런 것은 치과에 가면 간단히 해결되는 거에요."
"정말인가요? 몰랐어요. 감사합니다."
그녀의 조언을 듣고 당장 치과에 가서 치료를 받았다. 검게 변해 있던 치아가 감쪽같이 새 이처럼 보였다.
그때부터 나는 대인기피증에서 벗어나 자신감을 갖게 되었다.

They say pain leads to growth. A poet must write at least a hundred completed poems, compose a thousand drafts, and read ten thousand lines to finally share one worthy piece.And as Kim Nan-do once said,

"It takes a thousand times of trembling to become an adult."

Everyone carries a handicap. I had mine too. As a child, I lost a front tooth on the very day my grandfather passed away. By strange coincidence, the new tooth that grew in was black. From that day on, I stopped smiling in front of others. I avoided opening my mouth. One day, while serving as a Sunday school teacher at church, a woman who worked at a dental clinic noticed my tooth and said: "Teacher, since when has your tooth been like that? You know, this is something that can be easily fixed at a dentist's office." "Really? I didn't know that. Thank you so much."

Because of her kind words, I went straight to the clinic. Soon, the blackened tooth was restored─ bright and new, like the others. From that moment on, I was set free from my fear of people. Confidence returned. And I saw it: God had used even this pain to shape me─ to mature me.

누구나 잘하는 분야가 있다. 단 1도만 올리면 된다. 그런데 쉽지 않다. 그 1도는 하늘과 땅의 차이다. 죽을 만큼 힘들 때 그때를 참아내고 견디어 내는 것이 결국 나의 성장을 가져온다.

과학적인 지식이 없는 사람들조차 물이 얼거나 녹는 점이 섭씨 영도이며, 물이 끓는 점은 섭씨 100도로 알고 있다. 99도에서는 따뜻한 물은 될 수 있어도 끓는 물은 되지 못한다. 물이 끓어야 증기가 되고 무언가 확실한 원동력이 된다는 말이다. 그래서 1도 차이가 아무런 게 아니다. 삶에서 성공하는 이와 그렇지 못한 사람과의 차이는 단 1도에 있다. 뒤늦게 후회하며 이렇게 말한다.
"1도만 더 인내하고 노력을 했더라면. 단 5분만 더 참았더라면, 좋은 결과가 있었을 텐데."

아이슈타인이나 에디슨 등 천재적인 사람들은 남들보다 노력을 더한 사람에 불과하다. 그들이 천재로 인정을 받은 것은 그들이 열정과 인내가 다른 이들보다 한발 앞섰기 때문이다. 흔히 3심을 말한다. 3심은 초심, 열심, 뒷심이다. 처음에는 기분 좋게 출발하지만 작심 삼 일에 그치는 사람들, 남들보다 일찍 포기했기 때문이다.

Everyone has a field in which they shine. All it takes is just one more degree— a single step forward. But that "one degree" is no small thing. It can mean the difference between heaven and earth.

When life feels unbearable, it's in that moment—when we choose to endure— that growth takes root. That is when God begins to shape us deeply.

Even those without scientific knowledge know: Water freezes and melts at 0°C, and boils at 100°C. At 99°C, water may be hot, but it doesn't boil. Only at 100°C does steam rise— and steam, not warm water, moves engines. That final degree changes everything.

This is the same in life. The difference between success and failure often comes down to that one last effort. And so many later sigh and say, "If only I had held on just a little longer... just one more degree of patience, just five more minutes of endurance what breakthrough might have come?"

Einstein, Edison— they weren't born with magic. They simply persevered more than others. What made them seem like geniuses was not their talent alone, but the passion and perseverance to go that one degree further. Faith,

"99도까지 열심히 온도를 올려놓아도 마지막 1도를 넘기지 못하면 물은 영원히 끓지 않는다. 물을 끓이는 건 마지막 1도다. 이 순간을 넘어야 내가 원하는 세상으로 갈 수 있다."

세계적인 피겨 스케이트 선수인 김연아의 말이다. 김연아가 우승하기 위해 얼마나 혹독한 연습과 엉덩방아를 찧어야 했는지 아무도 모른다. 진정한 고수는 고난을 통해 더욱 성숙해지는 법이다. 마지막까지 고삐를 늦추지 않는다. 늘 평상심을 유지한다. 100도에 이르는 삶이 성숙한 삶이요 고수의 삶이다. 나보다 남을 낫게 여긴다. 늘 양보하고 나누는 마음이 크다.

99도로 자만하지 말자. 나머지 1도를 올리는 데 최선을 다하자. 삶의 질이 단 1도에서 결정되기 때문이다. 흔들리며 피는 꽃처럼 끝까지 내 자리를 지키자. 무엇이 나의 속을 뒤집어 놓는가? 나를 뒤흔드는 그 어떤 것이 있을지라도 참고 또 참자. 백도의 화려한 꽃을 피우기 위해.

You can raise the temperature all the way to 99°C, but if you fail to cross that last degree, the water will never boil. It is the final degree that makes it boil. And only by crossing that line can you enter the world you dream of."

These are the words of world-renowned figure skater Yuna Kim. No one truly knows how many times she fell, how many hours she endured grueling training to rise to the top. A true master is forged in hardship. They grow deeper, stronger, and never loosen their grip— even at the end. They remain calm under pressure. A life that reaches 100°C is a life of maturity. It is the life of a true master— one who considers others better than themselves, who yields, shares, and loves greatly.

Let us not grow proud at 99°C. Let us give our all to reach that last degree. For the quality of our life is decided there. Like a flower that blooms through trembling, hold your place until the end. Whatever shakes you— whatever stirs your soul or tries to break you— endure. And endure again. So that, in due time, you may bloom— a radiant flower at the boiling point of 100°C.

캐나다 원주민 사역을 하면서

이진종

내가 살고 있는 캐나다는 세계에서 두 번째로 큰 땅덩어리를 갖고 있다. 앨버타주만 해도 한국의 여섯 배나 면적이 크다. 캐나다는 사회보장제도가 잘 되어 있어 흔히 오대 천국으로 불린다. 앨버타주는 캐나다에서 서부 쪽에 위치하며 석유와 천연자원 등의 에너지가 풍부해 미국에서는 알래스카 주가 부자 주라면 캐나다에서는 앨버타 주가 부자 주로 세금도 없고 조용한 도시다.

캐나다에서 일조량이 가장 많은 도시가 바로 캘거리이다. 북미주에서 가장 안전한 도시이자 살기 좋은 도시에 늘 손꼽힌다. 세계적으로 유명한 로키산맥이 가까이 위치하여 사계절 관광객이 몰려온다. 밴프 국립공원을 위시해 주위에 네 개의 국립공원이 인접해 있고, 그중 루이즈 호수는 죽기 전에 반드시 가봐야 할 곳 상위 10위에 속한다.

밴프와 카나나스키스는 자연경관이 아름다워 지금까지 할리우드 영화 200편 이상이 이곳에서 촬영되었다. "닥터 지바고", "흐르는 강물처럼", "가을의 전설", "레버넌트" 등 마릴린 몬로, 브래드 피트, 레오나르도 디카프리오 등 세계적으로 유명한 배우들이 다녀갔다.

Serving Among the Indigenous Peoples of Canada
By Jin Jong Lee

Canada, the land where I live and serve, is the second-largest country in the world by land area. The province of Alberta alone is six times larger than South Korea. Known for its strong social welfare system, Canada is often counted among the top five "heaven-like" nations to live in. Alberta, located in the western region of Canada, is rich in energy resources such as oil and natural gas. If Alaska is considered the wealthiest state in the U.S. Alberta holds a similar status in Canada—with no provincial sales tax and a peaceful urban lifestyle.

Calgary, my city of residence, boasts the highest number of sunny days in all of Canada. It is consistently ranked among the safest and most livable cities in North America. With the majestic Rocky Mountains just a short drive away, it draws visitors from around the globe throughout all four seasons. The world-famous Banff National Park, along with three other adjacent national parks, surrounds the region. Lake Louise, one of the jewels of the Rockies, is often listed among the top ten must-visit places in the world before you die.

The natural beauty of Banff and Kananaskis has made them ideal locations for more than 200 Hollywood film productions. Iconic movies such as Doctor Zhivago, A River Runs Through It, Legends of the Fall, and The Revenant were filmed here—starring world-renowned actors like Marilyn Monroe, Brad Pitt, and Leonardo DiCaprio.

앨버타주에만 128개의 원주민 부족이 있다. 크게는 First Nation, Inuits, Metis 가 있다. 원주민과 백인 간의 상처는 깊어 복음화가 쉽지 않지만 한국인들은 얼굴 생김새도 비슷해, 그들이 쉽게 마음의 문을 열고 반가이 대하고 있다. 원주민들은 백인 목사가 있는 교회에 잘 출석하지 않는 편이다. 교회마다 창문이 깨져 있는 경우도 다반사로 새로 갈아 끼워도 깨지는 일이 반복되어 많은 교회가 어려움을 겪고 있다.

캐나다 원주민은 2006년 인구조사에 의하면 총 백이십만 명으로 전체 인구의 3.8%이다. 이중 퍼스트네이션은 70여만 명, 혼혈인 메티스는 40여만 명, 북쪽 에스키모로 알려진 원주민 이누이트는 5만여 명이다. 보호구역에 거주하는 82%의 원주민들이 실업자로 정부의 보조금에 의지해 살고 있다.

나는 매주 이곳에 들어가 기부받은 음식이나 헌 옷가지들을 들고 들어간다. 원주민들은 무료로 집을 배당받는다. 모든 학비와 장례식 비용도 무료다. 하지만 미래에 대한 준비 개념이 없어 저축한다든지 투자하지 않는다. 원주민 집들은 가족들조차 다 떨어져 산다. 하우스 넘버도 최근에 부착이 되었지 예전에는 원주민 집을 찾아가기도 쉽지 않았다.

In the province of Alberta alone, there are 128 distinct Indigenous tribes, primarily categorized as First Nations, Inuits, and Métis. The wounds between Indigenous peoples and white settlers run deep, making evangelism a challenging task. However, as a Korean, I have found that our similar facial features often help break down walls. Many Indigenous individuals feel more at ease and are open to engaging with someone who looks like them.

It is uncommon for Indigenous people to attend churches led by white pastors. In many communities, church windows are frequently broken—sometimes even after being replaced, only to be shattered again. This ongoing damage reflects deeper tensions and has made ministry difficult for many churches.

According to Canada's 2006 census, the Indigenous population numbers around 1.2 million, accounting for 3.8% of the total population. Among them, approximately 700,000 identify as First Nations, 400,000 as Métis (people of mixed Indigenous and European ancestry), and about 50,000 as Inuit, known for residing in northern regions. About 82% of Indigenous people living on reserves are unemployed and rely heavily on government assistance for their livelihoods.

I visit these communities weekly, bringing donated food and used clothing. Most Indigenous families are provided with housing free of charge, and the government also covers all educational and funeral expenses. Yet, there is a general lack of preparation for the future—saving money or investing is not a common practice. In many households, even close family members live separately. It was only recently that house numbers began to be assigned, which means that, not long ago, simply locating someone's home was a real challenge.

동인작가 글

  1800년대 캐나다 정부에서 약 100년 동안 원주민 자녀들을 서양식으로 교육하기 위하여 부모들의 동의 없이 강제로 기숙사 학교에 입학시켰다. 약 3세부터 15세까지 부모를 떠나 그들의 언어와 의복을 사용할 수도, 입을 수 없었고 말을 듣지 않으면 체벌은 물론 성폭력을 당하고 죽은 아이들이 상당수였다.

  그 위탁 교육을 대부분 천주교회와 연합교회 성직자들이 담당했기에 원주민은 물론 캐나다인의 분노가 컸다. 연방 수상도 공식으로 사과하고, 교황도 이곳 앨버타주를 방문해 공식 사과를 했지만 이미 상처를 받은 원주민들이었다. 교회 근처에서 발견된 수많은 아이의 유골 등이 캐나다 각주에서 발견되어 충격이 컸다.

  나는 이곳 카나나스키스 근처에 있는 스토니 나코다 원주민들을 방문한다. 이들이 믿는 원시종교가 있기에 이들이 교회에 와도 혼합된 종교 형태의 신앙을 갖는다. 한국 교회처럼 주일성수, 헌금, 섬김이나 봉사 개념이 거의 없다. 틴 에이저가 되면 쉽게 성관계를 하고 아기를 낳아 기르는 것을 보게 된다. 마약 복용이 심해 집단으로 마약을 하다 죽거나 병원에 실려 간다. 미래의 희망이 없다 보니 자살률도 매년 늘어간다.

Beginning in the 1800s, the Canadian government operated a system of residential schools for nearly a hundred years. Indigenous children were forcibly taken from their families—often without parental consent—and placed in these schools to be assimilated into Western culture. From as young as age three up to fifteen, they were forbidden to speak their native languages or wear traditional clothing. Those who disobeyed were subject to harsh discipline, and many tragically suffered sexual abuse—or even death.

These schools were primarily run by Catholic and United Church clergy, which led to widespread resentment not only among Indigenous communities but across Canadian society. Though the Prime Minister issued a formal apology and even the Pope visited Alberta to offer a public apology, the deep wounds remain. In recent years, the remains of countless children have been discovered in unmarked graves near former residential school sites across various provinces, shocking the nation and the world.

I minister among the Stoney Nakoda people near the Kananaskis area. Many of them still adhere to elements of traditional tribal religion, and even when they attend church, their faith is often a mixture of beliefs. Unlike Korean churches, there is little understanding or practice of Sabbath worship, tithing, service, or volunteering. Among teens, early sexual activity and teen pregnancies are common. Drug use is rampant—often leading to overdoses, hospitalizations, or even death. With little sense of hope for the future, the suicide rate among Indigenous youth continues to rise each year.

나는 매주 원주민들을 만나 복음을 전하고 기도한다. 그들의 상처가 쉽게 회복되지 않겠지만, 코비드 기간에 원주민 지역이 폐쇄되어 외부인들의 출입이 통제된 가운데에서도 나는 매주 방문하여 기부 음식을 집 앞에 두고 기도하고 돌아왔다. 내 재능 중 하나인 사진 촬영을 통해 지금은 원주민들의 프로필이나 가족사진을 촬영해 주면서 그들이 교회에 지속적으로 나와 믿음이 성장 되기를 기도하는 중이다.

캘거리 교회 연합으로 일 년에 몇 차례 원주민 마을을 방문해 원주민 자녀들에게 VBS(여름 성경학교)를 열고 Korean Culture night 을 통해 태권도, worship, 드라마 등 원주민 복음화를 위해 애쓰고 있다. 최근에 85세 된 캐서린 할머니가 소천을 했다. 마음이 아팠다. 손자인 카일은 연락이 안 된다고 딸인 폴라가 걱정한다. 툭하면 병원에 입원해서 기도해 달라고 연락이 왔는데, 최근에 도통 연락이 없으니, 마음이 좋지 않다.

아직 선교의 열매와 결과는 미미하지만, 코리언 교회와 사역자들의 역할이 매우 중요하다고 본다. 지금은 계란으로 바위 치기, 밑 빠진 그릇에 물 붓기 식이다. 하지만 큰 그림 즉 멀리 바라보고 지속적으로 하다 보면 그들의 삶이 변화되리라 본다.

Each week, I meet with Indigenous people to share the gospel and pray with them. Though their deep emotional and historical wounds are not easily healed, I continue to reach out in faith. Even during the COVID-19 pandemic, when Indigenous communities were on lockdown and closed to outsiders, I would still visit weekly—leaving donated food at their doorsteps, praying silently, and then returning home. One of the gifts God has given me is photography. I now use this skill to take portraits and family photos for Indigenous families. It is my hope and prayer that through these personal connections, they will feel loved, continue attending church, and grow in their faith.

Together with the Calgary Church Network, we visit Indigenous villages several times a year to hold Vacation Bible School (VBS) programs for their children. Through events like Korean Culture Night—which includes Taekwondo demonstrations, worship, and drama—we are striving to reach them with the love of Christ.

Recently, 85-year-old Grandma Catherine passed away. My heart was heavy. Her daughter Paula is worried because her son Kyle has gone silent and cannot be reached. In the past, she would often call asking for prayers when Kyle was hospitalized, but now there has been no word for some time. It troubles me deeply.

Though the visible fruits of this mission are still few, I believe the role of Korean churches and missionaries is vital. Right now, it may feel like striking a rock with an egg or pouring water into a bottomless jar. But I believe that with perseverance and a long-term vision, transformation will come. In God's time, their lives will be changed.

동인작가 글

둥지
이현경

세상을 향해 자유로이 날거라
따스한 햇살이 널 안아주고
부드러운 바람도 널 토닥인다

거센 폭우가 널 때릴 때
고민하지 말고
내게로 어서 돌아와

내 품 안에서 한숨 푹 자고
어둠이 물러가고 밝은 해가 인사하면
두 날개 펼쳐 자유로이 날거라

 이현경 선교사는 2007년 예수전도단을 시작으로 캄보디아에서 사역, 현재 청주 벧엘워쉽하우스 기도의 집 섬김이. 글로벌선교문학회 회원으로 활동 중이다.

The Nest

by Hyun Kyung Lee

Fly free, my child, to the open skies,
Where sunlight warms and softly lies,
And tender winds with quiet grace
Will kiss your cheeks and touch your face.

When storm clouds roar and lashes fall,
Don't be afraid—just heed my call.
Come swiftly back, don't stray too far,
My arms will hold you as you are.

Breathe deep and rest within my breast,
Where weary hearts are gently blessed.
When night has passed and light is near,
Unfold your wings—fly free, my dear.

벼랑 끝에서

이현경

바들바들 사시나무 떨듯
두 발은 어찌 할 바를 모릅니다

핏빛 울음을 토해 내며
지푸라기라도 잡으려
두 팔을 휘져어도
허공으로 곤두박질치는
돌맹이 되어 구르고 또 구릅니다

얼마나 굴렀을까
이제 죽었구나 체념하고
온몸의 힘을 풀고
그분 손에 맡길 때

겹겹이 나를 휘감았던
껍데기는 사라지고
핏빛 울음은 복사꽃 웃음 되어
눈부신 진주만 반짝입니다

At the Edge of the Cliff
by Lee Hyunkyung

Trembling like a quaking leaf,
My feet know not where to stand.

Blood-red cries spill from my soul,
Grasping for a thread, a strand.
Flailing arms through empty skies,
I fall—a stone in wild despair,
Tumbling down in silence deep,
Crashing through the hollow air.

How long I rolled, I cannot say,
Till hope was lost, and breath was still.
I loosed my grip, gave all away,
And placed my heart within His will.

Then all the shells that bound me tight
Unraveled, vanished, slipped from sight.
And tears once red turned blossom-bright,
A pearl of praise in morning light.

동인작가 글

미래의 어느 날 활짝 피어날 손주들에게
이현경

사랑하는 내 믿음의 자녀들아, 오늘은 너희에게 할머니의 삶 속에서 하나님께서 어떻게 역사하셨는지, 그리고 그분의 인도하심 속에서 어떤 기적과 은혜를 경험하며 살아왔는지를 들려주고 싶구나. 혹시 언젠가 너희도 믿음의 길에서 지치거나 흔들릴 때, 이 이야기가 작은 위로와 용기가 되어 주길 바라는 마음에서 말이야.

2007년, 제주 땅을 처음 밟던 날이 아직도 생생하단다. 설렘과 기대 속에서 시작된 나의 선교의 첫 걸음이었지. 이전까지는 그래도 조금씩이라도 월급이라는 수입이 있어서, 부족하더라도 나름의 안정감은 있었단다. 그런데 거기선 오직 주님께서 공급하시는 은혜로만 살아야 한다는 사실이, 어쩌면 작은 과자 한 봉지도 사 줄 수 없을지 모른다는 불안함이 나를 감싸기도 했어. 그럼에도 불구하고, 나는 주님의 은혜로 주어진 현실에 적응하며 그 시간들을 선교지 훈련이라 생각하고 묵묵히 걸어갔단다.

제주에서의 생활은 고된 선교 사역 틈틈이 자연과 함께였어. 고사리를 꺾고, 도토리를 줍고, 조개를 캐고, 미역을 따고, 이름 모를 풀들을 캐다 먹고, 수확 끝난 밭에서 이삭을 주웠단다. 귤나무에 몸살 난 귤을 따주며, 자연 속에서 건강하게, 그리고 감사함으로 살아갔지.

To My Grandchildren Who Will One Day Bloom in Full Glory

By Hyunkyung Lee

My beloved children of faith,

Today, I want to share with you a piece of my journey — how God has worked in my life and the miracles and grace I've experienced through His guidance. I write this hoping that, should you ever feel weary or shaken in your walk of faith, these words may become a quiet comfort and gentle encouragement to your heart.

I still remember the day I first stepped onto Jeju Island in 2007 — it is vivid in my memory even now. It was the beginning of my mission life, filled with excitement and hope. Until then, I had always had some form of income, however small, and that provided a bit of stability. But now, I had to live relying solely on the grace that the Lord would provide. At times, I was gripped by fear — what if I couldn't even afford a small snack to share?

Yet, I pressed on quietly, thinking of that season as a time of training in the mission field. I adapted to the reality I was given, depending on my thrifty nature and the grace God gave me each day.

Life in Jeju, in the midst of demanding ministry, was deeply intertwined with nature. I picked fern shoots, gathered acorns, dug for clams, harvested seaweed, ate wild herbs I could not even name, and gleaned leftover grains from harvested fields. I picked blemished tangerines from tired trees. And in all this, I lived healthily and thankfully, surrounded by the beauty of God's creation.

그리고 그 귀한 시간 속에 너희 셋, 하온이, 지음이, 환희를 차례로 선물로 받아 10년의 시간을 출산과 양육에 보냈단다. 어느 날 환희를 잉태했다는 소식을 들은 열방대학 목요 예배에서 나는 이런 기도를 드렸어. "주님, 선교지는 이제 끝인가요?" 하지만 곧 마음을 바꾸었단다. "주님, 네 아이 엄마로, 이름 없이 시골에서 예배하고 전도하고 중보하며 사는 것이 제 사명이라 하셔도 감사하며 살겠습니다." 그렇게 넷째를 주심에 감사하며, 주님 앞에 무릎 꿇었던 기억이 나.

결혼도, 선교도, 모두 주님 앞에서 내려놓아야 주시는 분이시란다. 결혼의 권리를 포기하고 나서야 나의 배우자를 만나게 해 주셨고, 해외 선교도 내려놓은 후에야 다시 길을 열어 주셨지. 그렇게 기쁘게 달려간 곳이 바로 캄보디아 몬돌끼리였단다. 그곳에서 뼈를 묻을 각오로 4년을 살다가, 급격하게 악화된 가족의 건강문제로 한국으로 돌아오게 되었단다. 두 달 후에 금방 다시 갈 줄 알았는데, 주님은 지금까지도 가는 걸 허락하지 않으시더구나. 그 대신, 4년 동안 주님은 우리 가족의 피로를 채우시고 먹이시고 입히셨단다.

And during that precious time, I was gifted with you three — Haon, Jieum, and Hwanhee — one after another. I spent ten beautiful years in the seasons of pregnancy, childbirth, and motherhood. I still remember a Thursday worship at University of the Nations when I first learned I was expecting Hwanhee. In tears, I prayed, "Lord, does this mean the end of my mission journey?" But soon, my heart changed. I whispered to God, "Even if You call me to simply be a mother of four, worshipping, interceding, and sharing the gospel in obscurity in the countryside, I will receive that as my calling with thanksgiving." I remember kneeling before the Lord, thanking Him even for the gift of a fourth child.

Marriage, too — like missions — had to be laid down before God before He gave it to me. Only after surrendering my right to marry did the Lord bring me my husband. And in the same way, only after I let go of overseas missions did He open the door once again.

That is how I joyfully stepped into Mondolkiri, Cambodia. I truly thought I would lay my bones there. We lived there for four years, ready to give everything. But then, due to sudden and serious health issues in the family, we had to return to Korea. At the time, I thought we would go back in just two months… but the Lord has not allowed us to return since. Instead, during these four years, He has clothed us, fed us, and gently restored our weary bodies and souls.

2023년엔 고성에서 쫓기듯 청주로 왔고, 선교관에서도 떠나야 할 상황이 되어 짐을 싸게 되었지. 막막한 그날, "선교사님, 갈 곳 구하셨나요?" 한 통의 전화가 걸려왔고, 급히 좁은 컨테이너 방을 보러 갔었단다. 그곳에서 나가야만 하는 상황이었기에 어쩔 수 없이 그곳이라도 가야겠다고 마음먹었는데, 바로 그 순간 또 전화가 왔어. 같은 분이 또 묻더구나. "아직 방 못 구하셨나요?" 상황을 설명하자 그분이 말씀하셨어. "사실은 한 달 전쯤 주님께서 선교사님이 2024년 12월까지 지낼 집을 마련하라고 하셨어요." 얼마나 가슴이 뛰었는지 몰라.

그렇게 갑자기 이름만 받은 아파트를 향해 남편과 둘이 이동했단다. 가는 길에 각자 기도했지. 나는 예전에 층간소음으로 고생했던 기억이 떠올라, '주님, 아파트가 무섭습니다. 1층이면 주님이 예비하신 집이라 믿고 들어가겠습니다.' 짧게 기도했단다. 그리고 도착해서 부동산 사장님을 따라 들어간 집이 바로 106호! 할렐루야! 기도한 대로, 1층이었지.

그날 오후 6시, 계약서를 작성하고 우리는 새로운 집으로 이사하게 되었단다. 그런데, 문제는 그 후였어. 너무 큰 액수의 월세에 마음이 눌렸지. 평생 이렇게 비싼 집에서 살아본 적도 없었고, 후원해 주신 분께 너무 큰 빚을 진 것 같았단다.

In 2023, we had to leave Goseong in haste and moved to Cheongju. Soon after, we also had to leave the mission guesthouse where we were staying, so we began packing once again. That day felt so uncertain. In the midst of it, I received a phone call: "Missionary, have you found a place to stay yet?" In a hurry, we went to see a small room made from a container. It was so cramped — barely enough space for our family — but since we had to leave the mission house that very day, I had resigned myself to move in there.

Just then, the phone rang again. It was the same person asking, "Still haven't found a place?" I explained our situation, and that's when the person quietly said, "Actually, about a month ago, the Lord told me to prepare a place for you to stay until December 2024." My heart pounded so fast — I couldn't believe what I was hearing. We only had the name of the apartment complex, but my husband and I decided to go see it. On the way there, we prayed separately. I couldn't help but recall a difficult time in the past when we had trouble with noisy neighbors in an apartment. So I prayed a short but sincere prayer: "Lord, I'm afraid of apartment living… but if it's a unit on the first floor, I'll believe this is Your provision and move in with peace."

When we arrived and followed the realtor into the building, we stopped in front of unit 106. First floor. Hallelujah! It was exactly what I had prayed for. That evening at 6 o'clock, we signed the lease and prepared to move into our new home. But then came a new struggle. The monthly rent was higher than anything we had ever paid before. I felt overwhelmed — not only by the cost, but also by the weight of the generosity from the person who had supported us. I began to feel as though I had received more than I could ever repay.

그때 기도 중에 주님이 물으셨어. "딸아, 섬김받을 때 뭐라고 하니?" "100배로 갚아 주세요, 라고 기도했어요." 하고 대답했지. 그 순간 아주 오래전 기억이 떠올랐단다. 20년 전, 이가 아파 치과를 못 간 간사님에게 월급 전부였던 8만원을 드렸던 기억. 그때 심은 씨앗이 지금 980만원으로 열매 맺은 것이구나!

나는 또 주님께 여쭸지. "주님, 100배면 800만원이어야 하잖아요!" 그런데 주님이 웃으며 말씀하시더구나. "그게 어제 일이더냐? 20년 이자가 붙었잖니~" 그 말씀에 온몸에 소름이 돋았단다. 주님의 계산은 정말 정확하셨어.

얘들아, 할머니는 지금도 그렇게 신실하신 하나님과 함께 '아자! 아자!' 하며 살아가고 있단다. 인생의 어려움 속에서도, 내 계획이 무너져도, 언제나 더 좋은 것을 준비하시는 주님이 계시기에 오늘도 믿음으로 살아갈 수 있어. 너희도 이 이야기를 마음에 간직하고, 어느 날 너희 삶에 마주할 어려움 속에서도 하나님을 신뢰하는 믿음의 사람으로 자라나길 간절히 기도한단다.

사랑을 담아 할머니가.

During that time, while I was praying, the Lord gently asked me, "My daughter, what do you usually pray when someone serves you generously?" I answered, "I always pray, 'Lord, repay them a hundredfold.'" At that very moment, a memory from long ago came flooding back. It was nearly twenty years ago, when I gave all I had — 80,000 won, my entire salary at the time — to a fellow staff member who couldn't afford to go to the dentist. I had almost forgotten about it. But now, I realized: the seed I had sown then had come back as a harvest — 980,000 won's worth!

I asked the Lord again, half-playfully, "But Lord, if it were truly a hundredfold return, wouldn't it be 8 million won instead?" And I could almost hear Him chuckling as He replied, "My dear, was that just yesterday? That was twenty years ago — I've added interest." A chill ran through my body. His math, His timing, His heart — all so precise, so tender.

My dear ones, even now your grandmother is living with that faithful God, cheering herself on each day with a little 'aja! aja!' (Let's go! Let's keep going!). Even when life is hard, even when plans fall apart, I've found peace in knowing that God is always preparing something better. I pray you'll treasure this story in your heart. And when you face your own hardships one day, may you grow to be children who trust God — completely, boldly, and joyfully.

With all my love,
Grandmother

작은 것들의 소중함을 잊지 않게 하소서

전 에스더

작은 바람 한 줄기에도 감사를 몰랐습니다.
햇살이 아침 창가를 두드릴 때도,
따스함이 기적임을 알지 못했습니다.

긴 병상의 시간 속에서,
한 걸음 내딛는 것이 소원일 줄이야.
한 모금의 맑은 물이 축복일 줄이야.
당연했던 모든 순간이 선물이었음을
이제야 깨닫습니다.

주님,
저에게 다시 주어진 이 하루를
소중히 여기게 하소서.
나뭇잎의 속삭임에도 기뻐하고,
작은 미소에도 사랑을 느끼게 하소서.

병상의 고요함 속에서 배운
감사의 마음을 잊지 않게 하시고,
살아있음에 감사하는 마음으로
남은 때를 소중히 살게 하소서

전 에스더 목사는 신유 사역, 교회사역을 하였으며 코칭심리학 박사 과정 중, 글로벌선교문학회 회원으로 활동 중이다.

Let Me Never Forget the Preciousness of Small Things

by Esther Jeon

I failed to appreciate the whisper of a gentle breeze.
When the morning sunlight knocked upon my window,
I did not recognize its warmth as a miracle.

Through the long hours of illness,
I never imagined that taking a single step would
become my heart's deepest wish,
That a sip of clear water could be a blessing.
Only now do I realize—
Every moment I took for granted was, in truth, a gift.

Lord,
Let me cherish this day You have given me once more.
Let me find joy in the rustling of leaves,
And feel love in the smallest of smiles.

May I never forget the gratitude I learned
In the quiet solitude of my sickbed.
And with a heart full of thankfulness for life itself,
Let me treasure each moment that remains.

22년의 친구, 내 안경

전 에스더

　　22년 전, 나는 총신 신대원에 입학하여 첫 관문으로 히브리어와 헬라어, 원어 공부를 시작했다. 공부량이 방대하여 눈 붙이고 잠을 잘 시간이 없었다. 아침 8시에 강의가 시작되어 오후 5시에 끝났고, 저녁을 먹고 나면 그날 배운 내용을 복습해야 했다. 다음 날 아침 쪽지 시험을 통과해야 했기에 새벽 1시까지 공부하고, 다시 새벽 3시 30분에 일어나 씻고 준비한 뒤 새벽 예배에 참석했다. 아침을 먹을 시간조차 없어, 김밥 한 줄을 사서 먹으며 화장하고, 다시 8시 수업에 들어가야 했다. 그렇게 눈을 감을 시간조차 없이 하루하루를 보내는 날들이 두 달이나 계속되었다.

　　때로는 양지 캠퍼스 부근에 있는 병원에 도움을 받기도 했다. 의사 선생님께서 총신 학생들이 공부하다 병원에 실려오기도 하는 것을 보면서 의대생들이 밤새워 공부하는데, 신학생들도 이렇게 열심히 공부하는지 알게 되었다고 놀라워 했다.

　　나는 당연히 육신의 병을 고치는 의사를 배출하는 과정이 그럴진데, 영혼을 섬기는 주의 종을 배출하는 신학교에서 이 정도는 당연한 것이며 이들보다 다방면의로 더 많이 준비되어져야 한다고 생각하면서 감사함으로 연약한 육체를 병원의 도움도 받아가며 감당했다.

My Glasses, 22 Years Friend
by Esther Jeon

Twenty-two years ago, I entered Chongshin Theological Seminary and began my journey with Hebrew, Greek, and biblical languages as my first challenge. The sheer volume of study was overwhelming, leaving barely any time to sleep. Classes started at 8 a.m. and ended at 5 p.m., followed by an evening of reviewing the day's lessons. Since I had to pass a quiz every morning, I studied until 1 a.m., then woke up again at 3:30 a.m. to prepare for the dawn prayer service. There was no time for breakfast, so I would grab a kimbap roll, eat while putting on makeup, and rush to my 8 a.m. class. For two months, I lived this way—without a moment to close my eyes for proper rest.

At times, I had to visit a nearby hospital near Yangji Campus for help. The doctor, seeing so many seminary students being hospitalized from excessive studying, remarked how surprising it was that theology students studied as intensely as medical students.

I thought to myself, "If such rigorous training is required to produce doctors who heal the body, how much more should we, as future ministers of God, be prepared in all aspects to care for souls?" With gratitude, I endured my frail body's struggles, relying on medical help when needed, knowing that this was part of my calling.

그러던 어느 날, 갑자기 눈이 잘 보이지 않게 되었다. 평소와 다름없이 생활하던 중이었는데, 글자가 흐려지고 사물의 윤곽이 뚜렷하게 보이지 않았다. 불안한 마음에 여러 가지 방법을 시도해 보았지만, 개선될 기미는 보이지 않았다. 결국 나는 스승님을 찾아가 상담을 받기로 했다.

스승님께서는 내 이야기를 조용히 듣고 나서, 잠시 생각에 잠기셨다. 그리고는 부드러운 미소를 띠며 말씀하셨다.

"사실 내 딸도 눈이 좋지 않아서 안경을 쓰고 있단다. 마침 내가 아는 안경원이 있는데, 거기서 한번 안경을 맞춰보는 게 어떻겠느냐?"

예상치 못하게 자신의 자녀처럼 따뜻한 배려에 나는 감동했다. 그뿐만이 아니었다. 스승님께서는 곧장 주머니에서 돈을 꺼내 내 손에 쥐여 주셨다.

One day, suddenly, my vision became blurry. I had been going about my daily routine as usual when, out of nowhere, the letters on the page began to blur, and the outlines of objects lost their clarity. A wave of anxiety washed over me as I tried various methods to improve my sight, but nothing seemed to help. In the end, I decided to seek counsel from my mentor.

My mentor listened quietly as I shared my concerns. After a brief moment of contemplation, he smiled gently and said,

"You know, my daughter also has poor eyesight and wears glasses. I happen to know a good optician—why don't you go there and get a proper pair of glasses made?"

I was deeply touched by his unexpected kindness, as if he were caring for me like his own child. But that wasn't all. Without hesitation, he reached into his pocket, took out some money, and placed it in my hand.

"이 돈은 지난번 집회에서 사례로 받은 것이지만, 사실 나는 이 돈을 내 것이 아니라 하나님께서 필요한 누군가를 위해 주신 것이라 믿고 있단다. 그래서 너를 위해 쓰는 것이 맞다고 생각했단다."

그 순간, 가슴이 뭉클해졌다. 단순히 안경점을 소개해 주시는 것도 감사한데, 직접 안경값까지 주시다니. 나는 그 돈을 받으며 고마움에 말을 잇지 못했다.

그 돈으로 맞춘 안경은 지금까지도 내 곁을 지키고 있다. 세월이 지나도 그 순간을 잊을 수 없다. 스승님의 넉넉한 마음 덕분에 나는 그때 어둠 속에서도 다시 세상을 선명하게 바라볼 수 있었다. 단순한 시력 회복이 아니라, 사람에 대한 신뢰와 따뜻함을 다시금 깨닫게 해 주었고, 누군가에게 베풀어야 할 따뜻함이 물질을 어떻게 사용할 것인가 하는 기준이 되었다.

이제는 나도 누군가에게 작은 도움이라도 줄 수 있는 사람이 되고 싶다. 22년이 지나도 그날의 은혜를 가슴 깊이 새기며, 오늘도 그때의 안경을 닦아본다. 안경 너머로 환히 피어오르는 햇살이 유난히 따숩다.

"This money was given to me as an honorarium from a recent gathering," my mentor said gently. "But I have always believed that such money is not truly mine—it is given by God for someone in need. And right now, I believe He wants me to use it for you."

At that moment, my heart swelled with emotion. It was already more than enough that he had introduced me to a good optician, yet he went even further by covering the cost of my glasses. Overwhelmed with gratitude, I accepted the money, unable to find the right words to express my thanks.

The glasses I purchased with that gift have remained by my side ever since. Even after all these years, I can never forget that moment. Because of my mentor's generosity, I was able to see the world clearly again—not just physically, but with renewed faith in people and the warmth of true kindness. His act of giving became a lasting lesson on how to use material blessings to extend love and support to others.

Now, I, too, hope to be someone who offers even the smallest help to those in need. Twenty-two years later, I still cherish that grace-filled moment as I gently clean my old glasses. Through the lenses, the morning sunlight shines especially warm today.

잃어버린 것과 얻는 것

전 에스더

삶은 때때로 우리가 계획한 길과 전혀 다른 방향으로 흘러간다. 보다 활력있는 미래를 꿈꾸며 전문코치 시험을 앞두고 있었다. 오랜 시간 준비해 온 시험이었고, 철저한 계획도 세웠다. 시험을 3일 앞두고 갑작스러운 교통사고를 당하며 모든 계획이 무너졌다. 앰블런스 차에 실려 병원으로 옮기며 간절히 바랐다. 기억이 가물가물 해 지면서도 입으로는 계속 뇌아렸다.

'제발 빨리 회복해서 시험을 치를 수 있게 해 주세요 네 하나님 아시죠!.

매정하게도 시간표가 늘 내 일정대로 움직여 주진 않았다. 교통사고 이후, 무릎 인공관절 수술까지 받게 되었다. 같은 수술을 받은 이들은 2주 만에 퇴원했지만 나는 그렇지 못했다. 수술 경과가 좋지 않아 33일 만에야 병원을 나설 수 있었고, 재활을 위해 다시 3개월을 입원해야 했다. 내 앞을 가로막은 것은 단순한 통증이 아니었다. 함께 준비했던 시험은 멀어져 갔고, 기대했던 기회들도 속절없이 사라졌다. 몸뿐만 아니라 마음도 함께 무너졌다.

What Is Lost and What Is Gained

by Esther Jeon

Life often takes us in directions we never planned. I had been preparing for a professional coaching certification, envisioning a more dynamic future. It was an exam I had worked toward for a long time, carefully planning every step. But just three days before the test, an unexpected car accident shattered all my plans.

As I was rushed to the hospital in an ambulance, I prayed desperately. Even as my consciousness faded in and out, I kept murmuring, "Please, Lord, let me recover quickly so I can take the exam. You know how much this means to me!"
But time has never moved according to my schedule.

The aftermath of the accident led to an even greater challenge—I had to undergo knee replacement surgery. Others who had the same procedure were discharged within two weeks, but my recovery did not go as smoothly. It took 33 days before I could leave the hospital, only to be readmitted for three more months of rehabilitation.

What stood in my way was not just physical pain. The exam I had worked so hard for faded into the distance, along with the opportunities I had eagerly anticipated. It wasn't just my body that suffered—my spirit crumbled as well.

어느 날 아침 초췌해진 마음으로 거울 앞에 섰다. 거울 속의 나는 예전의 나와는 전혀 다른 모습이었다. 몸의 균형은 무너졌고, 움직일 때마다 불편함이 따라다녔다. 하지만 내 마음만큼은 무너지지 않으려 애썼다. 나는 다시 걸을 수 있을까? 예전처럼 자유롭게 움직일 수 있을까?

결국 뒤틀린 몸을 바로잡기 위해 또다시 입원 치료를 받아야 했다. 단순한 재활이 아니라, 몸 전체의 균형을 되찾기 위한 과정이었다. 척추부터 골반, 무릎까지 정렬을 맞추는 치료가 이어졌고, 통증은 더욱 심해졌다. 침대에 누워 지내던 시간보다 몸을 움직여 다시 균형을 찾는 과정이 훨씬 더 고통스러웠다. 병상의 하루하루는 길고도 지루했다. 한 발짝도 앞으로 나아갈 수 없는 듯한 절망감이 밀려왔다.

어느 날 오후 거울속에 비쳐진 비틀린 내 모습을 보다가 문득 욥이 클로즈업 되는 걸 느꼈다. 이유도 모른 채 모든 것을 잃었고, 친구들로부터도 비난을 받으며 홀로 고난을 견뎌야 했다. 가장 가까운 아내도 입을 삐쭉이며 사랑한다고 고백하던 남편을 향해 말했다.
"다 끝났어요 뭐가 더 있어요? 차라리 그 하나님께 삿대질 하고 모른다 하세요. 나 당신 몰라 죽여 줘!! 고함치고 죽기나 하세요!"
거울 속에 선 여자가 머리 풀고 내게 달려들며 소리치고 있는 듯했다.

One morning, I stood before the mirror, my heart weighed down with exhaustion. The reflection staring back at me was nothing like the person I used to be. My body had lost its balance, and every movement came with discomfort. Yet, I fought to keep my spirit from collapsing. Will I ever walk again? Will I move as freely as before?

In the end, I had to be hospitalized once more—not just for rehabilitation but to restore my body's overall alignment. The treatment focused on realigning my spine, pelvis, and knees, intensifying the pain even further. The process of regaining balance was far more agonizing than the days I had spent lying still in bed. Each day in the hospital felt unbearably long and monotonous, and the despair of being unable to take even a single step forward loomed over me.

One afternoon, as I gazed at my twisted reflection in the mirror, the image of Job came sharply into focus. He had lost everything without understanding why, condemned even by his friends, enduring suffering alone. His wife, the one closest to him, had looked at the man she once loved and scoffed, "It's over. What else is left? Just curse God and die!"

In that moment, I saw a shadow of her in myself. It was as if the woman in the mirror let down her hair, lunged at me, and screamed those very words in my face.

시간이 지나면 짙은 어둠도 새벽 미명의 빛을 품고 찾아오는 것일까 어느 날, 문득 생각이 바뀌었다. '이렇게 시간을 흘려보내서는 안 된다. 지금 내가 할 수 있는 것은 무엇일까?' 몸은 자유롭지 못했지만, 생각하고 배우는 것은 가능했다. 세월을 헛되이 보내지 않기 위해 내 전공인 심리학을 더 깊이 연구하기로 결심했다. 그렇게 시작된 공부가 결국 나에게 다섯 개의 자격증을 안겨주었다. 나는 여전히 병상에 있었지만, 더 이상 멈춰 있는 사람이 아니었다.

잃은 것이 많았지만, 얻은 것도 있었다. 비록 건강을 잃고 기회도 잃었지만, 오히려 그것이 새로운 길을 여는 계기가 되었다. 욥이 고난 끝에 더 큰 축복을 받은 것처럼, 나 역시 이 시간을 통해 한층 더 단단해지고, 더 깊이 성장할 수 있었다. 절망의 시간이 곧 성장의 시간이었음을 깨달았다.

고통과 좌절의 시간 속에서도, 나는 배운 것이 있다. 우리 몸은 생각보다 강하다는 것, 우리의 의지도 그에 못지않게 강하다는 것. 1년 7개월째 긴 병원 생활과 긴 재활 과정이 나에게 가르쳐 준 가장 큰 교훈이었다.

Does even the darkest night eventually give way to the soft glow of dawn? One day, my perspective shifted. I can't let time slip away like this. What can I do right now? My body was still bound by limitations, but my mind remained free to think and learn. Determined not to waste these years, I decided to deepen my studies in psychology, my field of expertise. What started as a small effort eventually led me to earn five professional certifications. I was still confined to a hospital bed, but I was no longer a person stuck in place.

I had lost much, but I had also gained much. Though my health had failed me and many opportunities had slipped away, those very losses opened doors I never expected. Just as Job received greater blessings after enduring his suffering, I, too, found myself growing stronger and wiser through this time. I realized that what seemed like a season of despair was, in fact, a season of growth.

Through pain and hardship, I learned an invaluable lesson: our bodies are more resilient than we think, and our willpower is just as formidable. The long hospital stay and the grueling 17-month rehabilitation process became my greatest teacher, revealing the strength I never knew I had.

그 모든 과정 속에서 하나님의 깊은 뜻을 발견하게 되었다. 내가 견뎌온 시간은 단순한 고난이 아니라, 나를 새롭게 빚어 가시는 하나님의 손길이심을, 육체적인 연약함을 통해 나의 교만을 깨닫게 하셨고, 아픔 속에서도 감사할 수 있는 마음을 배우게 하셨다.

앞으로 나는 더 이상 연약함을 두려워하지 않을 것이다. 나의 삶이 온전하지 않을지라도, 하나님의 계획은 완전함을 믿는다. 나는 다시 걸을 것이다. 더 단단한 마음으로, 더 깊은 감사로 한 걸음을 내딛을 것이다.

나는 지금 휠체어에 의지하여 있지만 여전히 걷고 있다. 언젠가 이 모든 시간이 축복으로 다가올 것을 믿으며, 한 걸음 한 걸음 나아간다.

Through it all, I discovered the profound purpose of God. The time I had endured was not merely suffering—it was His hands reshaping me. Through my physical weakness, He humbled my pride. Through my pain, He taught me the beauty of gratitude.

From now on, I will no longer fear my weakness. Even if my life remains imperfect, I trust that God's plan is always perfect. And I will walk again—one step at a time, with a stronger heart and a deeper sense of gratitude.

For now, I lean on a wheelchair, yet I am still moving forward. I believe that one day, all of this will reveal itself as a blessing. So I press on, step by step, with faith.

동인 작가 글

믿음의 승리
정재식

눈물로 깨어진 기도의 밤이 지나
고요한 침묵 속, 주의 손길을 느낀다
깊은 상처 위로 은혜의 빛이 스며들고
그 사랑이 나를 다시 일으킨다

버림받은 듯 어둔 순간에도
주님은 결코 나를 떠나지 않으셨고
내려앉은 마음에 성령의 숨결 불어
절망은 소망의 씨앗이 되어 자란다

고난은 나를 짓누르지 못하고
오히려 나의 영혼을 빚어내며
가장 연약한 자리에서
그분은 나를 강하게 하신다

믿음으로 바라본 끝자락에서
나는 주님의 품 안에 웃고 있었고
그날의 승리는 먼 미래가 아니라
이미 오늘, 내 안에서 시작되었다

정재식 선교사는 필리핀 선교사로 라구나 진광교회 담임이며 미국 GGU 대학 아시아 지부 학장으로 섬기고 있다. 글로벌선교문학회 회원으로 활동 중이다.

Victory of Faith

by Jeong Jaesik

The night of tearful prayer has passed,
And in the silence, I feel His hand.
Grace seeps into my deepest wounds,
And His love lifts me up again.

Even in moments that felt like forsaking,
The Lord never turned away from me.
The Spirit's breath stirred my weary heart,
And despair grew into seeds of hope.

Affliction could not crush my soul;
Instead, it shaped and molded me.
In the place of greatest weakness,
He made me strong through His mercy.

At the far edge of faith, I looked ahead—
And found myself smiling in His embrace.
That victory I once thought far away
Had already begun in me today.

동인작가 글

나의 소명

정재식

불완전한 나를 부르신 주님,
나는 오늘도 묵묵히 걸어가네.
기도 위에 피어난 사명의 꽃,
그분의 음성이 내 삶의 정수가 되네.

고요한 침묵 속에 은혜는 깊어지고,
혼돈의 시간에도 감사는 자라나네.
나는 나의 뜻이 아닌,
진리의 자유 안에서 주의 길을 따르리.

누군가의 아픔에 연민으로 응답하고,
섬김의 자리에선 눈물로 낮아지리.
세월의 무게가 더해져도
주의 사역은 내 안에 멈추지 않으리.

눈물의 밭에서 기쁨의 열매를 거두며,
작은 순종이 하나님의 뜻을 이루리.
그 부르심 앞에 다시 고개를 숙이며,
나는 오늘도, 소명의 길을 걷는다.

My Calling

by Jeong Jaesik

The Lord has called this imperfect soul,
And still, I walk in quiet obedience.
A flower of calling blooms from prayer's root—
His voice becomes the essence of my life.

In sacred silence, grace grows deeper still,
And even in chaos, gratitude takes root.
I will not follow my own desire,
But walk in truth, in the freedom of His will.

I answer the pain of others with compassion,
And in the place of service, I choose tears over pride.
Though time weighs heavy upon my steps,
His ministry in me will never cease.

In fields of sorrow, I will reap joy's harvest,
For small obedience fulfills His great design.
Before His call, I bow once more—
And walk again the path of purpose.

고요한 순례자의 길
정재식

인생이라는 광야 속을 살아가다 보면 문득, 발걸음을 멈추고 싶은 순간이 찾아온다. 시끄러운 세상 한복판에서, 나를 향해 쏟아지는 수많은 목소리와 기대 속에서 정작 나는 누구인지 잊어버릴 때가 있다. 그럴 때, 나는 하나님께 나아간다. 아무도 없는 이른 새벽, 조용히 커튼을 걷고 말씀을 펴며 기도할 때, 내 안에 조용히 울리는 속삭임이 들려왔다.

그것은 누군가의 말이 아니었다. 나의 논리나 감정에서 나온 것도 아니었다. 설명할 수 없는 신비한 방식으로 마음 깊숙이 스며드는 하나님의 음성이었다. "내가 너를 부른다. 이 길은 네가 가야 할 길이다." 그 부르심은 요란하지 않았다. 오히려 더 고요했다. 그러나 고요했기에 더 강력했다.

그 이후로 나는 그 음성을 따라 걷기 시작했다. 이 길은 단순한 인생 여정이 아니었다. 그것은 영혼의 순례였다. 나의 인생의 삶은 그 부르심을 따라 걸으며 하나님과 나 사이에 나눈 사적인 기록이자, 삶의 지도였다.
"하나님은 항상 말씀하신다. 다만, 우리는 너무 시끄러워 듣지 못할 뿐이다."

The Quiet Pilgrim's Path
by Jung Jaesik

As I journey through the wilderness called life, There are moments when I simply want to stop. In the midst of a noisy world—Surrounded by countless voices, expectations, and demands- I sometimes forget who I truly am. And it is in those moments that I draw near to God. In the stillness of early dawn, When no one else is awake, I quietly pull back the curtain, Open the Scriptures, And begin to pray.

That's when I hear it—A whisper rising gently within me. It is not the voice of another, Not born of my own thoughts or emotions. It is the voice of God— Seeping into the deepest places of my heart In a mysterious and unexplainable way. "I am calling you. This is the path I have set before you."

His call was not loud or dramatic. It came quietly— Yet its stillness held a power that could not be denied. Since that moment, I have been walking in response to that voice. This path is not just the road of life— It is the pilgrimage of the soul. Every step I take in answer to that call Has become a private record, A living map of the sacred conversation between God and me.

"God is always speaking. We simply live in too much noise to hear Him."

하나님은 내게 목적지를 먼저 알려주시지 않았다. 오히려 "함께 걷자" 고 하셨다. 처음에는 그 뜻을 몰랐다. 그러나 점차 깨닫게 되었다. 순례의 길이 언제나 평탄했던 것은 아니다. 오히려 고난의 시기였다. 뜻대로 되지 않던 시간들, 기도해도 아무 응답이 들리지 않던 날들. 이해할 수 없는 상실과 아픔 앞에서 나는 낙심했고, 하나님의 침묵에 때로 분노했다.

그러나 돌이켜보면 그 시간들이 나를 단단하게 만들었다. 믿음은 고난을 피하는 능력이 아니라, 고난 속에서도 하나님을 붙드는 능력임을 배우게 되었다. 믿음은 흔들리는 것이 아니라, 흔들릴 때 더욱 매달리는 것이다.

내가 겪은 고통은 결코 헛되지 않았다. 그 속에서 나는 하나님의 성실하심을 체험했고, 내 신앙의 중심이 더욱 단단해졌다. 나는 강하게 주님께 질문하며 "주님 왜 응답하지 않으십니까?" 여쭐 때 주님은 침묵 가운데서 나와 함께 하시면서 모든 것을 인도하셨다. 이 깨달음은 내 인생의 방향을 바꾸었다. 순례자의 길은 고난을 피해 가는 길이 아니라, 그 고난 속에서 하나님과 함께 걷는 길이었다.

God did not reveal the destination to me at first. Instead, He simply said, "Walk with Me." At the time, I didn't fully understand what that meant. But over time, I began to see. The pilgrim's path was far from smooth― It was a season marked by hardship. There were moments when nothing went as I hoped, When I prayed but heard no reply, When loss and pain came without explanation. I grew discouraged. At times, I even grew angry at God's silence.

But looking back, I see now how those moments strengthened me. Faith, I learned, Is not the power to avoid suffering― It is the strength to cling to God within it. True faith does not mean we will not be shaken; It means we hold on all the more when we are. The pain I endured was not in vain. In it, I encountered the steadfastness of God. My faith became anchored, no longer shallow. I cried out to the Lord, "Why won't You answer me?" And though He remained silent, He was always there― Guiding me, step by step. That realization changed the course of my life.

The pilgrim's path is not a way around suffering, But a road walked with God through the suffering. A whisper rising gently within me. It is not the voice of another, Not born of my own thoughts or emotions. It is the voice of God― Seeping into the deepest places of my heart In a mysterious and unexplainable way. "I am calling you. This is the path I have set before you." His call was not loud or dramatic. It came quietly― Yet its stillness held a power that could not be denied. Since that moment, I have been walking in response to that voice. This path is not just the road of life― It is the pilgrimage of the soul. Every step I take in answer to that call Has become a private record, A living map of the sacred conversation Between God and me.

신앙의 여정에서 가장 힘든 것은 외로움이었다. 아무도 내 마음을 이해하지 못하는 것 같고, 기도의 응답도 들리지 않는 막막함 속에서 나는 깊은 고독을 경험했다. 그러나 그 고독의 한복판에서 나는 비로소 하나님과 마주했다.

　사람들의 관심과 평가, 인정에 기대 살아가던 내가 아무것도 기대할 수 없을 때, 나는 하나님 앞에 나 자신으로 섰다. 그 자리에서 하나님은 나를 새롭게 하셨다. 고독은 형벌이 아니었다. 그것은 하나님이 나와 독대하시는 시간이었고, 내 존재를 다시 빚으시는 시간이었으며, 세상의 소리로부터 내 귀를 씻어내시는 과정이었다.

　고독한 날일수록 더 깊은 성찰과 더 정직한 기도로 하나님께 나아간다. 누군가를 의식하지 않고, 하나님께만 집중할 수 있었던 그 시간은 나의 영혼을 정결하게 다듬었다. 고독은 결국, 하나님의 임재로 인한 충만함으로 바뀌었다.

Of all the trials on this journey of faith, Loneliness was the hardest. There were times when no one seemed to understand me, When even my prayers felt like they vanished into silence. In that overwhelming emptiness, I experienced a profound solitude— And in the heart of that solitude, I finally met God face to face. I had lived for the approval, attention, And affirmation of others. But when there was no one left to lean on, I stood before God—

Just as I was. And in that sacred place, He began to remake me. Loneliness was not a punishment. It was a divine appointment. A time for God to meet with me alone, To reshape my soul, To cleanse my ears from the noise of the world, And tune my heart again to His voice.

The lonelier the day, The deeper the reflection, The more honest the prayers. In those moments, free from the gaze of others, I focused solely on Him. And that quiet, unfiltered time with God Refined my soul. In the end, Loneliness was transformed—Into fullness, Born of God's very presence.

순례의 길은 철저히 개인적인 길처럼 보이지만, 사실은 공동체적인 여정이다. 하나님은 나를 부르셨지만, 나만을 위해 부르신 것이 아니었다. 그분은 내게 받은 위로와 깨달음을 흘려보내라 하셨고, 내가 걸어온 길을 다른 이들의 길에 등불로 삼으라고 하셨다.

그래서 나는 일상에서 작은 사랑을 실천하기 시작했다. 누군가의 말을 경청하고, 낙심한 이를 위해 기도하며, 말보다는 삶으로 하나님의 사랑을 증명하고자 했다. 때로는 말 한마디, 작은 선행, 그리고 따뜻한 침묵이 다른 누군가의 무너진 영혼을 붙드는 줄이 되었다.

나는 함께 함으로 기도의 대상이 생겼고, 함께 걷는 동역자가 생겼고, 내가 흘린 눈물이 다른 이의 회복을 위한 통로가 되었다. 하나님의 뜻은 언제나 '사랑'으로 귀결된다. 내 순례의 마지막 목적지는 하나님이지만, 그 길은 늘 이웃과 함께 걷는 길이다. 순례란 혼자 걷되, 결코 혼자가 아닌 길이기 때문이다.

나의 인생은 완성된 고백이 아니라, 계속 쓰여가는 순례의 기록이다. 하나님의 인도하심은 오늘도 내 발걸음을 이끈다. 나는 여전히 걷고 있다. 고요하지만 확신 있는 발걸음으로. 언젠가 그분 앞에 서게 될 날, 내 순례는 마침내 완성될 것이다.

The pilgrim's path may seem deeply personal, Yet it is profoundly communal. God called me― But not for myself alone. He asked me to pour out the comfort and wisdom I had received, To let the path I had walked Become a light for others.

So I began to practice small acts of love in daily life:Listening with patience, Praying for the discouraged, And letting my life―not just my words―speak of His love. Sometimes a simple gesture, A kind word, Or even a silent presence Became the lifeline for a weary soul.

In walking with others, I found those to pray for, Fellow travelers on this sacred road, And my tears became the channel Through which healing flowed into someone else's life.

God's will always leads to one destination: love. Though the end of my pilgrimage is God Himself, The way there is never walked alone. A pilgrimage is walked in solitude, But it is never a lonely road.

My life is not a finished confession, But an unfolding story ―

A record of the journey still being written. Even now, God continues to guide my steps. And I keep walking― Quietly, but with certainty. And one day, When I stand before Him, My pilgrimage will finally be complete.

친구

조복미

하늘하늘 이젤에
연초록 물감 뿌려
수채화를 그리시네

산들 바람 햇빛 실어
언 땅 뚫고 뾰죽뾰죽
새싹들 미소짓네

졸졸졸 개울 속
돌맹이 사이사이
송사리 숨바꼭질 하네

그리움 달래주는
정다운 나의 친구들
꽃초롱 웃어주네

푸릇푸릇 영혼에
청초록 사랑 뿌려
수채화를 엮으시네

조복미 목사는 상담심리를 전공 후 청소년 상담, 신학교에서 유아교육 개론 발달심리를 강의 함. 현재 찬양사역자로 주님을 섬기며 글로벌선교문학회 회원, 기독교 중독치유 클리닉센터가 세워지는 비젼을 품고 있다.

Friend

by Jo Bok-mi

On a gentle easel,
she sprinkles pale green paint,
painting a watercolor dream.

The breeze, carrying sunlight,
pierces the earth, and sprouting shyly,
the new buds smile.

Gently babbling, the stream,
between stones, between pebbles,
the minnows play hide and seek.

My dear friends, who soothe my longing,
smiling like lanterns of flowers,
their warmth lights my heart.

In the verdant soul,
she sows the tender seed of love,
weaving a watercolor of joy.

" 딸아 네 모습도 그리 아름답단다"

조복미

"그곳에 가면 살아있는 사람을 볼 수 있어요"라는 한마디에 강한 호기심이 발동했다
"네 살아 있는 사람요? 그 모습이 어떤 것인지 보고 싶네요!" 입에서 툭 터져 나왔다. 어느 날 " 목사님! 정말 살아 있는 사람을 보고 싶으세요 ? 가 보실래요? ""네! 보고 싶어요! "
이렇게 나는 밀알선교 합창단에 첫발을 딛게 되었다

밀알 합창단이 연습하는 곳은 고등학생 때 새벽 예배를 드리던 길가의 작은 교회였다. 목사님은 50십대 중반으로 사역에 매우 충성되고 내면은 성령으로 충만하게 채워졌던 분이셨다

어느 날 새벽 열 사람도 채 안되는 성도들이 드문드문 앉아 예배를 드렸었다. 예배를 마치며 아픈 사람은 앞으로 나와 안수기도를 받으라고 말씀하셨다. 나는 망설임 없이 앞으로 나가 코에 손을 대고 안수기도를 받았다 오랫동안 축농증을 앓던 나는 그날 이후 다시는 축농증으로 고통을 겪지 않았다.

"My Daughter, You Are Beautiful Too"
by Bokmi Jo

One day, someone said to me,
"If you go there, you'll see people who are truly alive."
That single sentence sparked a deep curiosity in my heart.
"Alive? What do they look like? I want to see that with my own eyes," I found myself saying aloud.
Then someone asked me,
"Pastor, would you really like to see someone alive in the Spirit? Do you want to come with me?"
"Yes! I really do!" I replied without hesitation.

That's how I took my first step into the Grain of wheat Mission Choir. The choir practiced in a small roadside church—the same place I once attended early morning services in high school. The pastor, then in his 50s, was a man deeply faithful to ministry and filled with the Holy Spirit.

One early morning, less than ten people had gathered for worship. As the service ended, the pastor said, "If you're sick, come forward and receive prayer."
Without hesitation, I stepped forward, touched my nose, and received the laying on of hands. For years, I had suffered from chronic sinusitis—but from that day on, I never suffered from it again. God healed me.

칠순을 바라보는 내게 새벽 예배시간에 병을 치료받은 신학교 1학년 그 시절로 나를 데리고 오신 뜻이 무엇일까? 주님 앞에 여쭙는 동안 내면에서 파장이 일듯 들리는 소리가 있었다
'그곳에 가면 살아있는 사람들을 볼 수 있어요'

어린 시절 새벽제단 흰돌교회에서 열심히 밀알선교 합창 연습에 참석하다 말로만 듣던 해외 찬양대행진 행렬에 올랐다 뜻하지 않은 감사와 감격과 다짐이 올라왔다. 나를 온전히 하나님께만 드릴 수 시간이 주어진 것이 얼마나 감사하고 감격스러운지 눈물이 났다.

이 순간부터 여러 가지 일로 분산되어 있는 내 마음을 주님께만 드리기로 결심했다. 오로지 내가 그분 안에, 그분이 내 안에 계시는 것 외에는 어떤 것도 사이에 두지 않기로 하였다. 첫날 조식에 들어갔다 맨 끝 떨어진 테이블에 앉았다 아침에 주님과 조용히 마주했다 마음은 평온하고 그의 음성은 어느 때보다도 달콤했다

Now, as I approach seventy, I ask the Lord:
"Why have You brought me back to this memory—my first year in seminary, when You healed me during that early morning service?"
As I waited before Him, I heard a gentle voice echo within my soul:"If you go there, you will see people who are truly alive."

I remembered those days as a child, practicing with the Milal Mission Choir at White Stone Church.
Eventually, I joined the overseas praise mission team I had only ever heard about. An unexpected flood of gratitude, awe, and deep resolve rose in me. Tears streamed down my face as I realized what a gift it was —to be given time to offer myself fully to God.

From that moment on, I made a decision: To give all of my scattered heart back to Jesus alone. Nothing else should stand between us—only He in me, and I in Him.
On the first day, I entered the dining hall and quietly sat at the very end of the table. In that silence, I met the Lord face to face. My heart was at peace, and His voice was sweeter than ever before.

2 주 동안의 찬양행진은 주님이 걸어가셨던 것처럼 낮고 소외된 말레시아의 조호바루와 인도네시아 바탐 극빈지역을 찾아가 2살 어린아이로부터 90세에 가까운 연세까지 구성된 250명의 찬양단이 3개 4개 팀으로 나뉘어 교도소, 양로원. 고아원 ,중독자마을, 극빈지역 교회, 특수 장애인 학교, 난민촌, 쇼핑몰등을 순회하며 준비한 찬양을 나누는 사역이었다.

이른 아침부터 늦은 저녁까지 계속되는 찬양대행진을 통해 주님은 내게 놀라운 은혜를 주셨고, 영혼과 육체를 만지시고 치유해 주시고 회복시켜 주셨다.

어린아이들이 밝은 미소와 맑은 영으로 찬양하는 모습을 보며 나는 감탄했다.
"주님 저 모습좀 보세요 "주님 저 모습이 너무 예쁘고 아름다워요 !!"

For two weeks, we journeyed like Jesus did— to the lowly and the forgotten, to the poorest places of Johor Bahru in Malaysia, and Batam in Indonesia. A choir of 250 people, ranging from 2 years old to nearly 90, was divided into three or four teams. We visited prisons, orphanages, nursing homes, rehabilitation centers, churches in the slums, special education schools, refugee camps, and even shopping malls.

From early morning to late night, we poured out praise wherever we went. And through it all, the Lord poured out grace upon grace. He touched our bodies and healed our souls. He restored us.

I saw little children praising God with radiant smiles and pure hearts. And all I could say was,
"Lord, look at them! Look how beautiful they are before You!"

그때 제 마음 가운데 들려오는 세미한 소리가 들려왔다
" 딸아 그리 아름다우냐?"
"네 주님 정말 오랜만에 보는 곱고 정결한 모습에요 정말 아름답고 사랑스러워요"
그때 주님께서 제 마음 깊숙한 곳에 속삭여 주시는 것을 느꼈다
" 사랑하는 딸아 내 눈에는 네 모습도 그리 아름답단다"
뜻하지 않은 주님의 음성에 나의 영혼은 환희의 빛으로 감싸였다 더 이상 땅이 아니었다 천국의 삶이 이럴거란 생각에 눈이 부셨다
"주님 감사해요 세상일로 분주하고 주님을 온전히 섬기지 못하며 살아온 저를 너도 아름답다 말씀하시니 감사합니다. 항상 주님 보시기에 아름다운 고운 영혼으로 섬기며, 주님의 딸로 설 수 있기를 바래요 저와 늘 함께 해 주세요"

오래 오래 눈물을 닦아내며 나를 일으켜 세워주시고 자존감을 회복시켜 주시는 주님의 따뜻한 손길을 느꼈다.

Then, in the depths of my heart, I heard a gentle whisper:
"My daughter, do you see how beautiful they are?"
"Yes, Lord," I answered,
"They are pure and lovely. It's been so long since I've seen such innocence."

And then He spoke again— softly, tenderly, deep within me:
"Beloved daughter, to My eyes, you are just as beautiful."
At those words, my soul was wrapped in heavenly light.
It was no longer earth—it felt like a glimpse of heaven.

"Lord, thank You," I cried,
"Though I've lived so busy with the things of this world, not giving You my full devotion, You still call me beautiful.
Please help me to always live as a beautiful soul before You, as Your daughter. Walk with me, Lord—always."

I wiped away my long-held tears. In that moment, I felt the Lord lifting me up, restoring my worth, and wrapping me in His warm embrace.

그리운 나의 어머니

조복미

어릴 적 나의 고향에는 5일 장이 섰다 장날에는 부모님들이 추수한 곡식들을 머리에 이고 지고하여 장에 내다 팔았다 그 돈은 쌀 보리 등 양식될만한 것들로 바꾸어 또다시 머리에 이고 지고 사 십리 길을 걸어 오셔야했다

국수를 한 그릇 사드시고 오면 좋았겠지만 그 돈마져도 아껴 보리 몇되 쌀 몇 되로 바꾸어 머리에 이고 배고픔을 참으셨다. 어머니의 고생을 생각하면 너무나 불쌍해서 가슴이 미어진다. 얼마나 힘드셨을까? 남편이 있고 가족들이 함께 살아도 어려운 그 가난한 시절에 초등학생 오빠와 미취학 어린 나 그리고 동생 어린 삼 남매를 데리고 어떻게 살아 내셨을까?

My Beloved Mother
By Cho Bok-mi

In my hometown, when I was young, there was a market every fifth day. On market days, my parents would carry the grains they had harvested, balancing them on their heads and shoulders, and take them to sell at the market. The money they earned was exchanged for rice, barley, and other food staples, and once again, they would carry them back, walking forty miles to return home.

How I wished they could have bought a bowl of noodles to fill their stomachs, but even that little money was saved, exchanged for a few pounds of barley, a little rice, and carried back, enduring hunger with stoic patience.

Thinking of my mother's hardships fills me with sorrow and sympathy, my heart aching. How difficult must it have been? Even with a husband and a family living together, how did she manage to survive those hard, impoverished years with an older brother in elementary school, a preschool-aged me, and two younger siblings? How did she carry us all through it?

내 바로 위의 오빠가 고생을 참 많이 했다. 산골에 눈이 내릴 때면 어머니는 불안한 나머지 어린 오빠를 데리고 땔감을 얻기위해 산으로 가셨다고 한다. 덕분에 헛간에 나무가 가득히 쌓여서 오히려 동네 사람들이 우리 집에서 땔감을 빌려 갔고 배로 갚아 주었다고 한다. 오빠가 우리 형제 중 키가 작은 이유는 그때 나무하느라 지게를 많이 졌고 일을 하도 많이 해서 못 자란 것이라고 한다.

어머니는 억척스럽게 사셨다. 우리가 아버지 없는 자식이란 티가 나지 않게 하시려고 애를 많이 쓰신 것이다. 명절이면 어린 시절 한참 유행하던 빨간색 팥죽색 골덴기지의 옷과 고무신을 사주셨다.

우리 형제들은 명절에나 받아 보는 그 선물이 좋아서 입어 보고 만져보고 하다. 머리 곁에 두고 잠들었다. 어린 자식들만을 데리고 홀로 사시는 어머니의 애로사항은 남자들이 해주어야 하는 농사짓는 일이었다. 대개는 놉을 얻거나 품앗이로 해결하였는데 그것이 쉬운 일이 아니었나 보다.

My older brother, just above me, endured a lot of hardship.

When it snowed in the mountain village, my mother, anxious, would take my young brother with her to gather firewood in the forest. Thanks to this, our barn would be filled with wood, and the villagers would borrow firewood from our home, repaying us with grain.

The reason my brother is shorter than the rest of us is because he carried a heavy load of firewood on his back so often and worked so hard that he didn't grow properly.

My mother lived with a fierce determination. She worked tirelessly to ensure that we, her children, would never feel like we were without a father. During holidays, she would buy us the red bean-paste colored corduroy clothes and rubber shoes that were in fashion when I was young.

We, her children, loved those gifts, especially since we only received them during holidays. We would try them on, touch them, and then fall asleep with them next to our heads.

Raising us children alone, my mother's difficulties were those that a man should have handled, like working the farm. Usually, she managed by borrowing labor or arranging for work exchange, but it wasn't an easy task.

어머니는 지혜로우셨다. 음식솜씨도 좋으셨지만 평소에 언제라도 손님상을 위한 음식 재료들을 준비해두셨다. 그런 탓에 장독대 소금 항아리 안에는 늘 굴비가 들어있던 기억이 난다. 어머니는 일꾼들에게 흡족하게 식사를 해주던 탓에 서로 일을 하려 했다고 한다.

이 세상에 단 한 분 나를 가장 잘 아시고 무조건적인 사랑을 주신 나의 어머니! 천국에 가신지가 벌써 25년이 지났지만 어제 일처럼 생소하게 어머니의 모습이 그려진다. 엄마! 감사해요! 어려운 삶을 견뎌내시고 내 나이 사십 중년이 될 때 까지 함께 하여 주셨던 것 그리고 나를 위해 기도해 주신 것 감사합니다!

"더 많이 안아 드리고 사랑한다"고 말하고 싶습니다

My mother was wise. She was not only a great cook but always prepared ingredients for meals for guests in advance. Because of this, I remember that the salt jar in the fermentation pit was always filled with dried yellow corvina fish.

My mother would feed the workers generously, and because of that, they were eager to work for her.

There is only one person in this world who knows me the best and gave me unconditional love — my mother! It has already been 25 years since she went to heaven, but her image still appears so vividly, as if it were just yesterday.

Mom! Thank you! Thank you for enduring such a difficult life and for staying with me until I reached my forties. Thank you for praying for me!

I wish I could hug you more and say I love you.

동인작가 글

초록벌레와 내 영혼

홍연옥

대문 옆 레몬나무에 달린
내 영혼의 작은 열매들은
초록 벌레의
사냥터 였나보다.

언제부턴가
푸르렀던 잎사귀
하나 둘 사라지고
몸통만 남은 가지에
아침 햇살 소리 없이
내려 앉고 있었다

홍연옥 선교사는 필리핀에서 교회개척 사역과 직업훈련원(IT) 사역,
싱글맘 사역(5병 2어)을 하고 있다. 글로벌선교문학회 회원이며 워십댄스 팀 에이레네와 오카리나 팀(시르오르)으로 활동중이다.

The Green Bug and My Soul
by Hong Yeon-ok

On the lemon tree beside the gate,
the little fruits of my soul
must have been a hunting ground
for the green bugs.

Somewhere along the way,
the once vibrant leaves
began to vanish, one by one,
leaving only bare branches.
And in the quiet morning,
the sunlight would softly
settle upon them.

언제쯤 앙상한 내 영혼
깨어날 수 있을까
날마다 옷 갈아입는
햇살의 비밀도 모른 채
넌 레몬 나무 곁에서
새곤새곤 잠들어 있었어

내 영혼의 슬픈 비밀이
새어 난 것일까
무심했던 발걸음 멈춰선
어느 포근한 아침,
대문 옆 레몬 나무에
파릇파릇 햇살 같은
새순이 미소 짓고 있었다

When will my withered soul
finally awaken?
Unaware of the secret of the sunlight
that changes its clothes each day,
you, by the lemon tree,
were sleeping so peacefully.

Could it be that the sad secret of my soul
has slowly leaked out?
On a warm morning,
my footsteps, once careless, came to a stop,
and by the gate, the lemon tree,
with its fresh green sprouts like sunshine,
was smiling.

동인작가 글

그리움의 무게

홍연옥

태양의 마지막 반짝임이
검은 바위 구멍 속을 훑고
낮아진 바람이
풀잎 사이를 훑고

그리움의 그림자가
검은 하늘 바다
반짝이는 물결이 된다.

계단이 있다면
오를 수는 있을까.
그리움의 무게는
어디까지 가벼워질까.

쥐어보아도 잡히지 않는
내 그리움은
검은 하늘
바다 고래가 된다.

The weight of longing
by Hong Yeon-ok

The last sparkle of the sun
scatters into the black rock crevices,
the wind, now gentle,
whispers through the grass.

The shadow of longing
becomes the shimmering wave
on the dark sky sea.

If there were stairs,
could I climb them?
How far would the weight of longing
grow lighter?

Though I grasp it,
my longing escapes,
turning into a whale
in the black sky sea.

오늘은 네 노트에서 네 글씨를 만져 보았다
홍연옥

너의 검은 눈동자가 하얀 막으로 채워져 갈 때
멀리 떠나는 기차에 오르고 있음을 직감했었단다
너무 아름다워 부르기조차 미안했던
열네 살의 미소, 열네 살의 꿈, 열네 살의 그리움,

아픈 몸으로 친구의 수업이 끝나길 기다리며
학교 앞 벤치에 앉아있던 너의 모습은 마치
온몸에 수천 개 쇠붙이를 달고 헉헉대며
마지막 플랫폼으로 들어서는 완행열차 같았어

정 많고 사랑스런 내 아들에게
용돈을 좀 더 줄걸
여행도 많이 갈걸
좋아하는 것 맘껏 하게 할걸
멋진 옷도 더 많이 사 줄걸
수많은 후회 속에 네 마지막 차가운 미소를
긴 비밀로만 남겨두고 널 품에 안았었다.

Today, I Touched Your Handwriting in Your Notebook

by Hong Yeon-ok

When your dark pupils began to cloud in white,
I knew you were boarding a train that would take you far.
You were too beautiful— even your name felt too
delicate to call aloud. Your smile at fourteen,
your dreams at fourteen, your longing at fourteen—
I still carry them.

Sick and worn, you waited on the bench
outside your friend's class. You looked like
a slow train dragging metal chains over
every inch of you, gasping into its final platform.

To my sweet, gentle son—
I should've given you more pocket money.
Let you travel more,
chase all the things you loved,
buy the clothes you liked.
Instead, I held you in silence, your last cold smile
buried like a secret beneath a thousand regrets.

널 보낸 후 교복 입은 아이들을 볼 때면
내 속에 활화산 같은 불이 피어나고
뿌연 안개 짙은 몽환의 숲길을 걷듯
오래 오래 길을 잃고 헤매곤 했단다

사진 속 네 미소가 피어날 때마다
엄만, 앞으로 어떻게 살아가야 할까!
감사의 열매는 어디서 찾아야 할까!
남은 아이에게 나눠줄 미소는 남아 있는가!
내 온몸에 피는 흐르고 있는 것인가!
텅빈 공허를 숨기고 살아가는 게 내 몫인가!
수억의 질문을 쌓아가며 밤을 지새웠단다

사랑하는 아들아!
어느 날, 너의 사진을 숨기고
어느 날, 너의 양말을 숨기고
어느 날은, 네 옷을 정리하며
불쑥불쑥 튀어나오는 네 편린들로
숨 막히는 고요와 눈물로 보내다
문득, 널 만날 날이 가까워져 온다고
억지로 나를 다독여 본단다.

Since you left, every time I see a child
in a school uniform, a wildfire rises within me—
I wander, like I'm lost in a mist-drenched forest
that never ends.

Each time your smile blooms from a photo,
I whisper: How am I to live on?
Where are the fruits of gratitude now?
Do I still have a smile to give your sibling?
Does blood still flow within this hollow body?
Is it my fate to carry this emptiness, unseen?
I stacked a million questions through sleepless nights.

My beloved son—
Some days, I hide your photo.
Some days, I tuck away your socks.
Some days, I fold your shirts
and let fragments of you leap out like sparks—
I face breathless silence, tears I can not stop.
Then one quiet moment, I murmur to myself:
The day I meet you again, must be drawing near.
And I press my hand against my trembling heart,
trying, just trying to hold myself still.

사랑하는 내 아들아!
오늘은 네 노트에서 네 글씨를 만져 보았다.
봉선화 꽃씨처럼 불쑥 튀어나온
네 말들과 네 몸짓들이 언어가 되고
슬픔이 아닌 감사의 시가 되어
내 영혼에 평안으로 내려와 주었구나

무척이도 보고 싶은 내 아들아 !
꼭꼭 묻어놓은 희망의 강줄기 차고 넘쳐
내 속에 묻은 너를 만나는 날
너에게 전하고 픈 한마디...
네가 환한 미소로 서성이는 그 문에서
너를 안고 노래하듯 들려주고 싶은 한마디
"사 랑 한 다
너무 아름다워 아까운 14살 내 아이야 !"

My dearest son,
today I touched your handwriting in your old notebook.
Your words, your gestures—
bursting out like balsam seeds—
became a language, and not of sorrow,
but a poem of thanks that descended
like peace upon my soul.

Oh, how I long for you. The river of hope I had
buried so deep overflows again.
On the day I finally meet the you I've carried inside—
there's one thing I wish to say. At that doorway,
where you stand with your radiant smile,
I'll hold you close and sing it into your ear—
one simple line, soft as a song:
I love you. My beautiful boy,
too precious to be only fourteen.

나만의 **책**을 만들어 드립니다!

소량 인쇄, 50권. 100권. 200권. 500권 이상 **소량 출판 가능**
시집. 소설집. 동화집. 수필집. 그림책. 자서전. 선교행전, 설교집
교보문고. 영풍문고. 알라딘 등에서 판매됩니다.

출판 형태 / 최고급 인쇄에서 세련된 편집까지

단체 회보 및 동인지 소량 출판 전문
해외 선교사 선교 보고서 <선교행전> 묶음
주일학교 노인학교 글모음집 동인지 출판
신앙 간증집, 기도문집, 가족문집, 전도편지
선교시집, 교회 역사자료집

국제문학사

대표 김성구

Ph.D., D.L. Pastor. Rev. Poet.

시인, 목사. 아동문학가, 철학박사, 문학평론가
서울특별시 광진구 광나루로15길 41. 101호(국제문학)

문의 010-3646-7271
이메일 kims0605@daum.net

『최저 비용으로 최고의 출판 실현』 | 국제문학사

신인작가 등단 작품 모집

종합문예지 《국제문학》에서는 가장 공정하고도 권위 있는 신인작가상 제도를 마련하여 아래와 같은 규정으로 참신하고 역량 있는 신인들의 작품을 모집합니다.
국제화 시대에 걸맞게 미래를 이끌어 나갈 신인들의 많은 응모를 바랍니다.

◉ 모집 부문

신인작가상
▶ 시 · 시조 · 동시 · 동요. 한시 5편 이상
▶ 동화 · 동극 2편 이상
▶ 수필 2편 이상
▶ 소설 · 희극 · 시나리오 2편 이상(원고지 80장 내외)
▶ 문학평론 원고지 100장 이내
▶ 체험수기: 신앙 간증, 목회, 사업, 생활수기 등

※ 꼭 첨부해야 할 것들 : 작품, 약력, 증명사진(2매, 스냅사진 1매),
주소, 연락받을 전화번호(작품 접수는 우편 또는, E-mail로 보내주십시오.)
당선작은 국제문학관, 국제문학공원 건립 시 우선 설치할 수 있습니다.

■ 접 수 : 3월, 6월, 9월, 12월 말까지 / 접수는 수시로 받습니다.
  * 원고는 가능하면 이메일로 접수 합니다.

◉ 규정

▶당선자는 기성문인으로 대우한다. 추천 3심제 통과는 신인작가와 등등 대우한다.
▶응모작품 끝에는 주소와 본명을 명기하고, 겉봉에는 '○○부문 응모작품' 이라 명기한다.
▶시상식은 1년에 1회 실시한다.

◉ 보내실 곳

서울특별시 광진구 광나루로 15길 41 (102호) 계간 국제문학사
문의전화 : (02) 465-7271 . 010-3646-7271
   E-mail : kims0605@daum.net

국제문학사

2025 Global Mission Literature Association
사막길을 걷는 이에게 들려주는 노래
Rose of the Desert

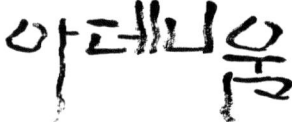

글로벌선교회문학회 동인지

아데니움

지은이 | 글로벌선교회 문학회
만든이 | 김성구
만든 곳 | 국제문학사
만든 날 | 2025년 9월 1일

등 록 일 | 2015.11.02.
등록번호 | 제2020000026호
주   소 | 서울특별시 광진구 광나루로 15길 41(102호)
전   화 | 070-8782-7272
전자우편 | Email: kims0605@daum.net

값 20,000원

ⓒ 판권 저자 소유 2025 글로벌선교회 문학회 Printed in Korea
이 책의 저작권은 저자와 국제문학사에 있습니다.
무단 복제를 금합니다.